To. Duncan  40p

25/12/89

Jack in the Spirit

Best wishes,

Jack.

John Woodson

By the same author:
Jack in the Pulpit
Jack in the Navy

'Jack's rich tapestry is woven with the vibrant colours of life in the raw, and the sombre lines of intermittent tragedy. But through it runs the golden thread of his unsentimental belief in the goodness of human nature as well as his faith in God.'

NAVY NEWS

'A humorous and at times moving recollection of his years as a "sin bosun".'

NEWCASTLE JOURNAL

'Jack brings to life a cast of doughty characters.'

MORPETH GAZETTE

'Brimful of rib-tickling tales.'

NORTHUMBERLAND GAZETTE

'A jolly good read and a real tonic.'

CLIVE JACOBS 'SUNDAY' BBC RADIO 4

Jack in the Spirit
a vicar's ghostly tales

Illustrated by Henry Brewis

Bridge Studios
Northumberland
1989

First published in Great Britain in 1989

by Bridge Studios,
   Kirklands,
   The Old Vicarage,
   Scremerston,
   Berwick upon Tweed,
   Northumberland TD15 2RB.

   Tel: 0289 302658/330274

ISBN 1 872010 00 8

Typeset by EMS Phototypesetting, Berwick upon Tweed.
Printed by Martins of Berwick

Foreword

'You're a lying toad, Jack Richardson. These stories are not true; they just cannot be.' Thus spoke my friend with honest candour. I may be a toad and if so, I hope that a beautiful, young princess will come along and kiss me; but a lying toad . . . no way. I admit to a certain amount of embroidery but I have sought to keep the truth of the stories intact. 'A ghost eating a bacon sandwich? Never in this world,' my friend and sceptic Bill Hume doubted. May I refer him to the Bible . . . if he has one.

Recently I was in Killin by Loch Tay. Standing in the information centre of the Scottish Tourist Board waiting for the manageress, Christine, to conclude complicated booking arrangements for an elderly and rather fussy American, I idly picked up a book of ghost stories. Flicking through its index I saw that one chapter dealt with Baleakin House. As I have also written about that spectre-ridden dwelling I purposely avoided reading that chapter, although sorely tempted to do so, as I wished to avoid the charge of plagiarism.

All my stories are basically true and are original. Most ghost stories seem designed to shock and terrify. I have written mine to entertain and at the same time to challenge but certainly not to frighten any reader.

How did my interest in the supernatural come about? It was, I believe, both inherited and instructed. I have a naturally enquiring mind which cannot be content with mystery; it seems to really activate when faced with any problems – scientific, theological or spiritual.

I owe a great deal to my mother. She was governess to the children of a High Court judge who went to India on circuit duty. He took his family and my mother to this country of mystery, ancient customs and many gods.

A convinced and dedicated Christian, my mother had a great sympathy with the Hindus. Her curious mind constrained to seek a closer understanding of their ways and faiths. She claimed, and correctly so, to have been the first British lady ever to set foot in the forbidden, sacred city of Peshuwar and by doing so she literally took her life in her hands. She told us tales of exquisite hospitality of maharajahs; of living on the edge of jungles, threatened by a tiger; the Taj Mahal in moonlight and of the Khyber Pass. She told us of the mystic rites and ceremonies carried out by families of condemned men who were very often hanged with a pig's skin over their heads.

She used to sit with the holy men of Hinduism while they explained their practice of palmistry. They taught her how to read palms, tell the future in cards and even to read tea-leaves. She loved and trusted the Indians and could make herself easily understood by them in their own language.

I'm sure that a great deal of this rubbed off on to me and that to an even greater degree to my twin sister. I am convinced that she has psychic powers. However, I enjoy my involvement with the spirits and I'm sure that there is much inspiration to be gained from them. One certainty is that we are never alone!

I'm not quite sure about spiritualism and have an open mind on the subject. Many of my friends are spiritualists but I do not think that it is right to conjure up spirits of loved ones. I feel that if they need to come to you then they will. Did Saul really see Samuel's shade or was it, as the

Witch of Endor cried, 'an evil spirit'?

> From all ill dreams defend our eyes;
> from nightly fears and fantasies.
> Tread underfoot our ghostly foe
> that no pollution we may know.

From *Compline* translated by J. M. Neale.

Good reading . . . and who is that behind you?

Jack

Purposeful Phantoms

Bill is my friend even though in his frank devotion to me he equated me with a 'lying toad'. He carries considerably more bulk than I do; the great, overweight bull-frog. We sat in his office and I could clearly distinguish his shapeless hulk through a screen of cigarette haze. He is a fount of knowledge, being an expert on a wide divergence of subjects; Robbie Burns, lay-lines and standing stones, King Arthur, whose table Bill maintains is the plateau upon which Edinburgh castle stands adjacent to Arthur's seat, Northumbrian pipes, Gaelic history and the Reformation.

However, he was confused. Despite his profound ecclesiastical knowledge, which warred continually with his professed agnosticism, the realm of the spirit left his 'rational thinking' irrational. 'What's that little b..... doing there?' he asked. He had shown me a snapshot. His dentist friend had been on a cruise up the River Nile. At Luxor, a twenty-eight feet high statue of an Egyptian pharaoh had toppled and now lay cradled upon two mighty stones. The dentist desired to photograph it. He stood well back in order to get the full length within the scope of his camera. Apart from palm trees and the statue there was no other thing within focus or sight and certainly no living person, either Arab or non-Arab.

The dentist told this story. 'When we reached Cairo I took the film to a chemist to be developed. When I returned to collect the prints the shopkeeper thrust them into my hands, refused any payment and begged me to leave his premises as quickly as possible. To effect this he pushed me from the shop and bolted the door behind me to prevent my re-entry. When I reached my hotel I looked at the prints.'

Bill continued with the story. 'After his return to his home at Hexham, the dentist and his family experienced a number of extraordinary and unfortunate happenings, and they finally came to the conclusion that the shapshot of the fallen Pharaoh was jinxed. He told me of his fears.

'Give me the photograph. I don't believe in hoodooism,' Bill told him.

'Please do take it, but for your sake burn it.'

'Ah, fiddlesticks,' Bill had replied. Bill took it.

'Jack, I have kept that snap for two years and I'm convinced that there is something weird about it. Will *you* take it?'

I laughed. 'What's frightening you, Bill? Scared of a snapshot. I thought you were a materialist and had no time for silly suppositions,' I jibed.

'I'm not scared; no b..... fear. Have a look at it,' insisted Bill.

I looked at it. In clear outline lay the recumbent pharaoh fringed by a few palm trees. Nothing weird about that, but standing near to the head of the fallen statue stood a figure no more than three feet in height. It was arrayed in the full vestments of a high priest of Re, the god of the sun and creator and maintainer of all living things. All the adornments and accoutrements of his elevated office were clearly discernible. He was so priestly that I am sure that he would not have appreciated Bill's previous description of him as 'that little b.....'.

'Someone has been playing hokey-pokey with the negative,' I suggested.

'No. My friend has had the negative examined by two experts and they both declare that the priestly figure was on the original exposure and has not been super-imposed,' insisted Bill as he handed me a magnifying glass. I examined the print very closely. No one could have appeared in such imposing and magnificent vestments and not be noticed by the photographer.

'Take it. I want to be rid of it. Think what you like,' said Bill unabashed, 'and check up on your Egyptian religions.'

'That's kind of you. Who wants enemies when they have you? I'll take it and see if I can find anything else about it.' I replied as I placed it carefully between the pages of a book.

'I don't believe in ghosts,' continued Bill, 'but if there are any they can only be justified if there is any purpose in their manifestations. I can see no purpose in that little Gippo putting himself on that film.'

Bill was full of inconsistencies. 'I would agree that it would be easier to accept the appearances of spirits if we can see the need or purpose behind their activities. There are, in my opinion, some hauntings that appear on the surface to be purposeless,' I agreed.

'Like what?' asked the agnostic.

I had to think quickly. One specific example sprang to my mind.

It was a glorious summer's day, when the air was warm and the sunshine beckoned from outside and rebuked indoor procrastination. I had visitors.

'Let's climb up to the castle,' suggested the young daughter of my visitor. The castle stood in ruins topping a motte and bailey immediately opposite to the vicarage. It had a short but turbulent history. Developed from a Saxon keep, which is still in a fairly good state of preservation, it was ultimately destroyed by Alexander III of Scotland in 1318 AD.

In June, 1215, King John of England was forced by the barons to accept the Magna Carta. Then, too late, he regretted this and decided to punish the barons who had supported the Charter. On St. Thomas' Day, December 21st, 1215, John and his French mercenaries came down the valley and laid siege to Mitford Castle. The incumbent of the castle at that time was John Mitford who was renowned for his exceptional height. He was alleged to be six feet seven inches tall and was known as 'Long John'. He and his men stoutly defended the castle. King John in order to demoralise the defenders, set fire to the church into which the women and children had fled for sanctuary. The leaping flames and agonised cries of the perishing served only to stiffen Long John's resistance, until a French soldier threw a battle axe which split Long John's skull. With his death all resistance ceased and the castle was surrendered.

Shortly after the First World War a 'dig' was organized by a team of student archaeologists. At the west end of the ruined castle they uncovered a grave as well as the foundations of what had obviously been a chapel. In the grave was a skeleton of a man who had been six feet seven inches tall and had a fractured skull.

'I hope you're wearing the right shoes for the going is rather steep and rough,' I said to the mother. Puffing and panting we entered the ruins from the west, and made for the Saxon keep. Two people were already there; an elderly man and a woman about sixty years old.

'Oh, how pleased we are to see you,' said the strangers almost simultaneously.

'And we are pleased to meet you,' I answered, 'and to see that you have found a nice quiet spot. We won't intrude. Cheerio.'

'No, wait, please,' the woman begged.

They had obviously intended to have a picnic. A rug and a cloth had been laid on the grass in the cool shade of the ruins but the food was still in its containers.

'Don't go. We want you to take us out of here,' said the woman.

Puzzled, I asked: 'Why? Aren't you feeling well?'

The woman shivered despite the warm air. The old man stood up with a little difficulty. 'We had a most pleasant afternoon here in the shade,' he began, 'and as my wife was preparing to lay out the picnic I looked over yonder.'

He indicated with his finger the remains of the old chapel and the place where a simple stone slab covers the remains of Long John.

'I saw a man standing there,' he said.

'From the village or the farm, perhaps?' I ventured.

'No,' replied the woman, 'He was exceptionally tall and was dressed in a fashion of hundreds of years ago.'

'Did he move or speak?' I asked.

'He moved,' the old man said; 'We both saw him and grew alarmed as he walked towards us.'

'Could it be a trick of the light?' I queried.

'Definitely not. He came within six yards of us, paused and then slowly walked back to where we had first seen him

and then – he vanished.'

'You're quite sure?' I asked.

'Sure enough to be scared to go past that end. Is there another way down from here?'

'Well, there is but it's rather steep and we'll have to negotiate a fence,' I told them.

'Anything as long as we don't have to go past that end.'

That was my story. Bill had listened patiently.

'I like to feel that there is a purpose behind apparitions but could find none here. If it was Long John why did he appear and frighten two elderly people? From what we know of his life he was not a man to deliberately upset people.'

'Has he been seen since?' asked Bill.

'Not since but others claim to have seen him before this episode. I still can't find an answer to why he appeared,' I remarked.

Bill stubbed out his cigarette end in his saucer and immediately began smoking another weed. He gazed pensively at me. When Bill thinks, one never knows the outcome.

'Jack Richardson; you're a b....... lying toad,' he said in his usual eloquent vocabulary. 'Do you really expect me to swallow all that?'

'What about your photograph, you inconsistent heathen,' I countered.

I kept that photograph for over a year showing it to several people for their comments. It stirred and challenged their imagination but none could give a satisfactory solution other than it was in fact a phantom. Finally I felt increasingly uneasy about it and threw it on the fire!

Purpose behind hauntings is often declared by the words and actions of the wandering spirit.

In my daughter's bedroom there was a seeker. A vague form would appear at the foot of her bed and softly call, 'Henry, Henry.' Christine was young and unafraid.

Paul, my son, had several experiences which suggested that *his* nightime prowler was also seeking for something or someone. The ghostly intruder entered his room through a window leaving no indication of his entry in the deep snow outside. Awakened by an icy blast which blew from his now-opened window, Paul heard the church clock strike four o'clock. The moonlight was reflected into his room from the white canopy of snow and cast an eerie glow about the walls.

'Dad; the man walked from the window to the wardrobe

doors knocking over my bedside table as he moved. He flung open the wardrobe and began to throw my clothes to the ground. Then he left the room to go along the passage. When I heard him coming back I dived beneath the sheets and did not surface until daybreak.'

That was the first of the marauder's many intrusions. They only ceased when he rudely shattered the most important time of the week. Malcolm sat with me awaiting the football results from the television. Newcastle United's result would be crucial to the relegation struggle. Immediately before the results were due there was utter confusion reverberating from Paul's bedroom. 'He's there Malcolm.

7

You take the back stairs; I'll dash up the front,' I cried as we both hurried out.

The noise of the upheaval persisted right up to the moment when we flung open the door. Then there was absolute silence. The room was in total disarray and no one was there. When we returned to the television viewing the results had been given and we had missed them. This was indeed sacrilege. 'Right; he's gone too far this time,' I said, 'I'll fettle him for good. Hold the fort, Malcolm.'

I hurried to church. I prayed. I collected my clerical robes and returned to the vicarage. After the exorcism we were no longer troubled by that destructive, though disturbed spirit. For six weeks he had searched for something. Did he find it? Was the exorcism effective? Who knows?

All manifestations do not have a disturbing or frightening purpose. All are not seeking or destroying.

I preached. A lady member of the congregation claimed that she saw a withered right hand appear from beneath my surplice sleeve and a black skull cap form on my head. The lady was a stranger to the parish and had never been in that church before.

'A previous vicar died either forty or four hundred years ago. I cannot get the message clearly. His service in the spirit world is to inspire the occupant of your pulpit. You'll never be lost for inspiration as long as you are in this parish,' she told me. I considered that I must be on a good wicket with someone doing the running for me!

The following morning I called on my churchwarden whose wife was the church organist. I had not told them or indeed anyone else of the woman's alleged sighting for I was more than a little sceptical.

'Youngsters today do not display the same respect to their elders as we had to when we were young,' said the organist. 'Boys had to doff their caps to the vicar and girls had to curtsey, but then, I was afraid of the vicar.'

'Afraid? Surely not afraid of your vicar,' I remarked.

'He was a weird, little man. He died forty years ago. He

always wore a black, skull cap and he had a withered right arm.' He certainly fulfilled his purpose for I felt that I was truly inspired when in that pulpit. I wonder if subsequent incumbents have so benefited from his expert and of course well-informed knowledge, for I had the pulpit renewed after dry-rot made it unsafe!

An amazing positive purpose is evident in these stories. The school building had stood abandoned for a few years. The powers-that-be eventually decided to create a library and lecture rooms for adult education in the premises. The builder's workmen toiled for weeks and when the work was completed on a Friday it was decided to call in cleaners to clear away the rubble in order that the rooms could be ready for the installation of bookshelves and desks. When the women cleaners arrived to carry out this work on the Monday morning they found that the place was spick and span and all Bristol fashion. No one had been in the building over the weekend and the locks and door bolts were still in closed positions. Equipment began to arrive over the next few weeks but every morning the place was found to be thoroughly cleaned and packing rubbish arranged outside ready for disposal. The weekend before the opening of the building as a library the stone stairs leading to the upper rooms were still wet from the industrious scrubbing of a tidy natured spirit.

It was a kindly black dog which accompanied pedestrians climbing the hill from the church on dark, wintry nights.

It was a caring, conscientious, Polish airman who had perished when trying to land in fog after a raid on Nazi Germany who talked down living airmen endeavouring to land in fog at an airfield in Warwickshire.

Purposeful phantoms; yet many still remain beyond our understanding. As St Paul so rightly wrote.

'Now we know in part; but then shall we know, even as also we have been known.'   (1 Corinthians ch. 13 v. 12)

Mort Farm

The fireside was cheerful and the kettle sang its praises. A pair of antique china dogs guarded the mantlepiece as a family of cats ruled the room. Three cats occupied overseeing positions on the sideboard, one nondescript moggie lay in a cardboard box which was intended as a maternity unit and Tom, the patriarch of them all, surveyed his domain from the centre of the table.

This table supported the old lady's fruit cake, an enormous cheese and a number of large mugs the stains of which indicated the beverages for which they were normally used. Donald and Robert drank tea, their mother preferred hot water and as a non-tea drinker I was privileged to have coffee. However my status as vicar of the parish entitled me to a china cup and saucer which after use would be replaced in the corner cupboard in the parlour. Don lifted his elbows from the huge oak table.

'Come on, Bob; milking time,' he demanded. Don was large and pleasantly illiterate and had a vocabulary of his own formed from his farmyard associations. Once when watching women swimming on my television he licked his lips and remarked, 'By, they're grand heifers.'

Bob was his opposite. He spoke in a more refined way and did all the necessary paper work and form-filling. He might think that the swimmers were grand heifers but would not comment.

The byres were next to the earth netty which was a friendly, communal affair having two seats and a lesser one for a child. There were only six cows and no modern intrusions such as milking machines.

'Them's the best milking machines,' boasted Don as he extended his huge, knarled hands. The farm was not connected to an electricity supply so milking and mucking-out had to be performed in daylight, hence their television viewing at the vicarage. The house used paraffin lamps and all cooking was done on an open fire. The large kitchen seemed to be larger when the two men had departed. Old Emma replenished her mug with hot water, broke off a lump of cheese and began to nibble.

'Any news from the village, vicar?' asked Emma.

I brought her up-to-date.

'How is it that your lads have never married?' I asked her.

'Bob never had a lass. He's sensible; got his feet on the ground. Looks after his old mother,' she began.

'What about Don?'

'He did have a lass. She was no good for him. She had ideas.'

'Ideas?' I questioned.

'Aye; she wanted to do things to this house. I told her it was good enough for us and had been for grandad and so was good enough for Don. She was a bit of a nuisance but I got shot of her,' possessive Emma proclaimed.

As she was speaking I heard a terrible noise coming from upstairs. An abusive row had started, apparently in the room above the kitchen. I could hear two distinct voices, male and female. The argument reached such a pitch that I feared there would be violence. I was greatly alarmed and not a little embarrassed. Emma seemed to ignore it.

'I didn't know you had guests. Have you got lodgers?' I asked.

'Lodgers? No. Why?' she asked.

'Can you hear that noise?' I persisted.

'There's nobody here except us,' she insisted.

'Nobody? Then who is upstairs?' I demanded.

'Oh, you might as well know. It's just the ghosts,' she said in a matter-of-fact tone.

'Ghosts?' I queried.

'Aye, but I'll stop them.'

She went to the passage door, opened it and shouted in a voice that would awaken the dead, 'SHUT UP.'

There was silence. The voices ceased.

'Come off it, Emma,' I said, 'there is someone there.'

'No,' insisted Emma, 'just the ghosts.'

She sipped her watery beverage.

'They argue every day and when I get tired of them I yell. They soon shut up,' she informed me.

'Just a minute,' I objected, 'I heard voices; human voices. Convince me. Let me see for myself.'

'Right,' she said in agreement. She knocked Tom from the table and led the way on a tour of inspection. The

passage was like a tomb. Stuffed creatures abounded. A pheasant that missed the shoot stood for the rest of time in a dusty glass case, entombed alongside a ferret which undoubtedly would have eaten its eggs; an owl clutched a mouse in its claws – a meal it would never devour – and a duck which had escaped the oven only to spend its time directing its discoloured beak towards the front door which never opened. Propped against the door was a collection of sticks and crooks with heads carved from the horns of rams. Wellington boots fell upon each other at the base of the stairs. No carpet softened our tread as we mounted the stairs and the upper landing was large enough to pen two dozen Canada geese – but the droppings there were those of pigeons.

We went into Emma's room. It was neat. The bed dominated the scene and stood high and immense. It sported brass knobs. A feather mattress lay on top of another. A thick eiderdown was partially covered by a patchwork quilt. I reckoned that she would require a rope ladder to facilitate ascent. A tilley lamp stood on a bedside table and her bible beside it. A large oval photograph, faded with age, depicting the enveloping whiskers of her father and the high-necked, buttoned blouse of her frowning mother, hung above the fireplace. There was no sign of anyone living or dead.

The quick and the dead were also absent from Don's room. The only thing related to death was the sheep-skin rug which met his feet every morning. Bob's room overlooked the byres and the only pervading essence was the rich, hair-growing stench of cow manure.

There were three other rooms all of which faced north. They were filled with boxes, trunks, jumble and a further collection of stuffed animals so tightly packed that there was little or no room for inhabitants, either of this earth or from the shades of Sheol.

We came downstairs. Emma guided me into the parlour. It smelt of mothballs. The heavy curtains kept out the daylight. The mats were home-made of cut up old skirts, coats and woollies and known as 'proggy mats', and they muffled our tread. A horsehair sofa had been rendered unsafe through the activity of woodworm. The corner cupboard held the matching replicas of the china cup I had been using. A number of large framed prints hid most of the faded wallpaper; Stag at Bay; a ploughing team with an advertisement for seed potatoes across the corner and,

Father surprisingly, St. Mark's Square, Venice. 'Now,' said Emma. 'look there.' She pointed to the floor on the narrow side of the room. I looked. I could see nothing extra-ordinary. 'See how the floor boards do not meet the skirting board? There's quite a gap,' she pointed out.

'Natural shrinkage,' I suggested.

'Shrinkage, yes; but not natural. It's warmer in the kitchen; let's go in there,' she said as she began to move.

Tom was emulating his natural enemy by gnawing at the cheese and the pregnant cat was nourishing the young within her feline womb with fruit cake. They must have thought that it was their birthday. Emma dispersed them as she had the argumentative ghosts. She stirred the fire.

'Years ago a farmer lived here,' she began. 'He and his wife had no children. His wife was crippled after a tussle with a bull and could only walk aided by crutches. Let's make you some more coffee, that's cold.'

My china cup overflowed into the saucer. Bob came in from the byres and poured a mug of stewed tea then sat down to listen and occasionally nod in assent to his mother's saga of the floorboards.

'The farmer's wife disappeared. He gave it out that her leg had become totally useless and a sister had taken on the care of her. Immediately after her departure he installed a young kennel maid as his resident bitch. After a space of about two years he sold the farm to my grandfather, and went to live in Westmorland.'

Robert sipped like an emptying sink and Tom attacked the cheese again. The high-water mark in Emma's cup ebbed and I sank a pleasant mouthful of coffee.

'Grandad noticed that the floorboards in the parlour left a gap beside the wall. He and uncle George lifted them to re-lay them and found beneath them the grisly remains of the farmer's wife. There was little left apart from the bones. No doubt rats had eaten the flesh. The stink must have been terrible; a kind of retribution for a ghastly murder. I wonder that they stayed as long as two years. The farmer was arrested, tried and hanged. He tried to implicate his paramour but she turned Queen's evidence and her words were sufficient to condemn him to the gallows.'

'Well,' I said, 'did your grandad replace the boards?'

'Of course,' she replied, 'and made a good job of it. Within a week he was really dumbfounded. Despite his care and skill the floorboards had again left the wall. With George to help him, they again removed the boards and searched beneath them. They found nothing, as they expected to find nothing. The police had done a good job with their investigations, but before Grandad replaced them for a second time he involved the police. They dug about and even uplifted the boards of the passage. Who else could be missing? A lover perhaps. They found nothing. The boards were again replaced and well and truly positioned with two new planks adjoining the walls. Within a week they had shrunk again. They have been left like that ever since.'

'Do you ever sense any uneasy atmosphere in the room?' I eagerly enquired. Robert spoke up.

'I do.'

'He's psychic,' informed Emma, 'always has been. Just like my sister Abigail. She used to see things.'

Evidently he had not seen enough of the inside of the byres for Don came steaming in with a load of manure on his boots.

'What's this then boy,' he addressed his brother who was junior to him by eighteen months. 'There's work to be done out there. Oh, well, let's have a cup of tea seeing as how the vicar's here. Did mother ever tell you of the shrinking floorboards?'

Underground Movements

The colliery is now closed. Deep in the earth its black arteries no longer pulsate with the throb of the coal-cutting machines or the clashing of the hewers' picks on the coalface. No longer does the conveyor belt distribute its life. All is dark and still and dead!

Not quite dead. Here and there the silence of this abandoned tomb is broken by the sound of scurrying rats left to their inevitable fate as the murky darkened waters rise from the crumbling floor. Now and then portions of the roof cave in to echo and re-echo their mournful requiem along the deserted, worked-out seams. The stench of death drenches old workings and abandoned tools.

The dead have uninterrupted reign. Screams are heard as the victims relive their agonies; the fatal fall of stone; the devastating explosion from damp gas; the crunch of the conveyor belt as it tears limb from body and the crash of the cage in the shaft. Many of these sightless spectres are doomed to roam those channels of darkness and death until the final judgement when the sea and the mines will give up their dead.

In days when men toiled and sweated to wrest the coal from the bowels of the resisting earth two men sat together on their honkers, that is upon their folded legs. Their backs rested against wooden pit-props while the water dripped unceasingly from the rugged roof the props supported. The only illumination was provided by the lamps fitted to their hats. Looking shaftwards they could see the distant glow of electric lights and further away along another working the dim, individual cap lamps of their workmates moving about like fireflies.

They were eating their bait, that is their packed lunch. Packed in tin boxes to prevent rats from eating the provisions while their coats hung on nails driven into the props, were the regular jam sandwiches and in the narrow necked tin bottles was cold tea. It was bait time.

'Geordie,' Bill's voice was almost inaudible as a set of laden tubs was pushed along by a couple of putters, 'That was an awful thing that happened to Ken Carter. Do you know the full story?'

'Aye. Well; about as much as anyone does,' replied

Geordie.

'They say that Ken'll never come down the pit again. Is that right? You're his marra; you ought to know,' said Bill.

'He cannot come down He's physically disabled and he's terribly disturbed mentally,' informed Geordie.

'Hae ye been te see him?' asked Bill.

'Oh; aye; nearly every day. He disna get alang to the club noo, though. The doctor says he has te lay off the beer,' sighed Geordie, as if this last restriction was a fate worse than death.

'That's aawful,' commiserated Bill.

They sipped at their cold tea and nibbled at the bread and jam.

'Ken was in fore shift,' resumed Geordie, 'he was pumper on the old galleries.'

A pumper is one with the responsibility of maintaining the numerous water pumps scattered about the galleries and workings. Ken had been employed to check on a set of pumps especially making sure that the main bearings were sufficiently greased.

'He had difficulty getting along a stretch of workings owing to a previous fall of roof which had partially blocked the way but he had to reach this big pump as it had been damaged,' began Geordie.

'Aye; I knaa the place. I used to work in there years ago. I hated it. The seam was only twenty inches high and aawful wet. The coal was nee good and we packed up alang there,' remarked Bill. 'Ken reached the pump alright and he had checked the grease when he thought he saw a shadow. He knew that no one should be along there so he lifted his head to see who the intruder might be,' related Geordie. 'There staring him in the face was a grimacing skull! Its sightless eye-sockets seemed to mock Ken. In the darkness he could not distinguish any form or body outside the arc of his cap-lamp. The skull came nearer, leering with jaws full of grinning teeth. Then as he watched, unable to move, the head seemed to take on an identity. It was Ken's mate of years ago who was killed while attending to pumps

17

along that very passage.'

Bill and Geordie drained their tea cans. Bill was beginning to feel a little weird and wished that he had never broached the subject, at least while down in the pit, but Geordie continued.

'Ken was found wandering by the next shift. He had not reported at the shaft at the end of his shift and the under-manager sent a deputy and a couple of safety men to look for him. When found, he was babbling incoherently and had obviously experienced a great shock. They took him to Ashington Hospital.'

Geordie had not come to the end of his tale yet but paused for a moment. 'Isn't it time we got cracking?' suggested Bill.

'When I'm finished talking aboot Ken. He was my marra, ye knaa,' insisted Geordie. 'Twenty-four hours after Ken was brought to the surface, the colliery disaster siren sounded. There had been a fall of stone in the main gallery just near to the old working where Ken saw the skull. I was there at the time and got hurt. I was off for a month with a bad back but reckon that I was lucky as four men were killed in that fall. Ken maintains that his dead mate had appeared to him to save his life.'

'Good for him,' said Bill.

'Well; maybe not. The very next day after that fatal accident Ken suffered a stroke. He can walk a little now but his right side is affected and his speech is slurred and that's why he doesn't like to meet too many people. He plays dominoes and cards with me but rarely speaks and I know that he's still seeing that skull in his nightmares. Bella, his wife, is patient with him and if care and affection will cure him then Bella's the one to do it.'

I was relating the story of Ken's visitation to a retired miner. He listened intently. He was a kindly man. His legs were bowed as was his back as a result of nearly half a century of toil and sweat in low, wet seams which ran beneath the North Sea. He remembered the days when miners' clubs were places of hard drinking by hard workers and a pint of beer could be bought for four pence. He welcomed the trend that was changing the clubs into family establishments where wives and sweethearts can now enjoy the entertainment and beverages in what was previously a male-orientated domain.

'I saw a ghost down the pit!' he said to me as I finished telling my story of Ken.

'Were you scared?' I asked.

'Far from it. I was intrigued. In fact I felt challenged,' he said.

'Challenged?' I queried.

'What I saw tugged at my heart strings. After I first saw it I wept,' he admitted, 'I told my wife after I came home from back shift. I had been married for six years and had a laddie aged four. He had been to the lavatory which was across the back lane.

' "Fasten my buttons for me, Dad" he asked.

'I looked at him. I thanked God for him. I put my arms around him. His short trousers fell about his legs and suddenly he was more precious to me than ever before.

' "What are you doing, Joe, Fasten the bairn's pants up for him," my wife said.

' "Sit down Sarah," I said, "and listen to this. I saw a young lad down the pit today. I reckon that he would be only eight or nine years old."

' "What was he doing down the pit?" asked Sarah.

'Well, in a way he wasn't there. I saw his spirit.

' "Joe, what are you saying? You saw the ghost of a little laddie?"

'Yes, Sarah. There's no doubt about it. It's where I always eat my bait. Today I was on my own. My marras were having an argument about football. They're United-mad but one supports Sunderland. I was fed up with them and moved a few yards away for the sake of peace. Then I saw him. A pitiful, little lad, indescribably dirty and dressed in a canvas covering rather like a smock. His face was begrimed but sweet and he seemed to be pleading.'

' "For what?" asked Sarah.

19

'I don't know but I'll find out. I hope he comes again!' Joe continued talking to me. 'I saw nothing for two weeks. Then in a space of five days I saw him four times. He always approached me and looked so pitifully at me. There was nothing scarey about him.'

Joe leaned heavily on his stick and continued, 'On his fourth appearance I spoke to him.

' "What can I do for you, Lad?"

'He actually smiled; a shy yet happy smile of apparent relief.

'In answer he walked away a few yards and pointed to the ground, then vanished. That night as I was washing in the tin tub in front of the fire; no pithead baths in those days; I told Sarah.

' "I believe that he is buried there. It's an old pit. It was working before the 1830s. I'm going to dig tonight." '

His hesitation made me impatient. 'Carry on Joe,' I requested.

'I found his body, or to be more correct his bones. They were not deep, with only a covering of coal dust and slag. He must have been pitifully small. The overman brought the manager who suggested that we cover up the bones again. I resisted. I felt that the lad had appeared to me so that he could be buried on consecrated ground. I felt that he had put his trust in me and that I would be letting him down if I did not protest. Irrational perhaps, but I wanted his bones to feel the warmth of God's sunshine again before a Christian burial. The coroner gave me permission to take the responsibility for the funeral arrangements. We took him into church and sang "The Lord's my shepherd".

'I placed a stone over his grave in the churchyard. I named him after the pit and added the inscription:

BORN 19th CENTURY
ADOPTED 20th CENTURY
One of God's sunbeams

'I look forward to meeting him in the next life. I'll know him and I know he will love me. Canny laddie; he's at rest!'

Kate

In a churchyard; in a churchyard,
where the myrtle boughs entwine;
there midst roses and pretty posies
lies my darling Clementine.

So in song and legend the daughter of the American prospector lies in sweet repose unless of course she walks to haunt her lover who soon forgot her and kissed her little sister!

With even greater, more lavish extravagance, nature has combined all her beauty to pay tribute to one of the most renowned beauties of the seventeenth century. Kate lies, not in a churchyard or even in consecrated ground but, although there are no myrtle trees, the birch and ash, the oak, elm and rowan tree shade her sepulchre which was hewn out of the solid crags at Harnham. The songs of the birds reflect the happy tunes that so melodiously at one time sounded from the lips of Kate. The green turf is the successor to that which yielded lightly to the gentle tread of her lithesome feet. Perched high the knoll of trees partially obscure her last resting place and the passing seasons gently stamp their passing so as to enhance nature's tribute. Had Shelley seen this peaceful and secluded sepulchre I feel sure that he would have applied his words, 'Half in love with death to be buried in so sweet a place'. Instead this epitaph offers its warning from the grey stone wall of above Kate's narrow bed;

> 'My time is past as you may see.
> I viewed the dead as you do me;
> Or long you'll be as low as I
> and some will look on thee.'

Her time is past but what ardent passions and religious fervour filled her short span on this mortal coil. Deeply devout, unyielding in her beliefs, beautiful in character as well as in features she died, imprisoned in her own home at the age of thirty-six and in the year of Our Lord 1670.

'You must not gaze at ladies, Emma. To watch them passing by; yes, but never when they are eating,' spoke the anxious mother who was herself endeavouring to have a sly and perhaps prolonged peep at the elegant Catherine Babington.

'But, Mum, isn't she lovely? She must be the most beautiful lady in the whole wide world, next to you of course, Mummy. If I mustn't look how is it that others can? Just look at this crowd,' responded Emma. Her mother had not realized the vastness of the gathering of people about her all intent on watching Kate eat a pie.

'What's all this obstruction?' angrily demanded the beadle from Durham Cathedral, 'There is no room for my horse to pass. Clear a way I tell you.'

No one yielded. The beadle stretched his legs above the stirrups and so was enabled to see over the heads of the onlookers. He saw a most beautiful lady in a public eating place in Saddler Street but irritation had dulled his eye to beauty. He spurred his horse into the crowd. There were howls of protest. Emma fell to the ground and the beadle was unhorsed. His language was of non-ecclesiastical purple. Picking himself up from the cobble stones while the crowd resumed their gaze upon Kate, he retreated to the main door of the cathedral as if seeking sanctuary. Looking back he espied the Dean's lean, long figure amongst the crowd and he wondered what the Church was coming to! He lodged a complaint.

The result of his moaning which was born of the sin Pride, which in his case had been injured, was without precedence and was rather startling for it restricted the rightful liberties of a lady whose only crime had been that of being born beautiful. The city fathers and magistrates issued an order.

'Dame Catherine Babington is forbidden, from the date of this order, to eat pies in any public eating place within the boundaries and confines of Durham City. She must use a private room that she be not stared at of the people, for a complaint was raised against her in that she ate a pie with such delicacy and grace in a public eating place thereby causing a motley crowd to gather in such great numbers as to cause an obstruction in Saddler Street.'

Emma hoped that she would grow up to be a beautiful lady and be able to eat pies with such grace. Well, eating pies would be sufficient reward for growing up whether with delicacy or just the ability to eat them!

Jim Humpish turned the car from the main road that led towards the ancient battlefield of Otterburn to a field track in obedience to the direction on an obscure finger-post. Its single word 'Harnham', which means the 'homestead in the horn (or corner) of land', was waging a losing battle against the outgrowing hawthorn hedge and the tall wayside weeds and grasses. Imprisoned in parallel cart tracks the car had a bumpy passage. 'Oh; it's a gated road,' remarked Jim as he sighted a five-barred gate straddling the track.

'That's O.K. Jim. I'll open it,' I offered.

I pushed at the gate. It was stubborn. I applied my shoulder to it and felt my spinal discs popping and slipping. I huffed and I puffed until Jim shouted. 'It opens towards you, Jack; and try the other end. There's a chain there!' Sheepishly I followed his bidding while two tups made sheeps-eyes at me. Easily the gate swung as intended and as I walked backwards with it, my right foot squelched into a generous supply of natural manure! I could feel the oozing richness of it flowing like a high tide into my shoe. The culprit lay with its fellow bovines chewing its cud and eyeing me with baleful derision and perhaps a smirk on its beastly features. The car passed through. I closed the gate. 'Hey; you can't get into the car with that load of sweet violets on your shoe,' protested Jim, an ex-submariner who being a sailor didn't know the nutritious benefits derived from organic matter. I hobbled to a clump of grass and began to remove the offending substance and its accompanying odour.

No further gates challenged our progress or my skill at opening them but a very steep incline of one in four suddenly rose before us. Jim reached for a periscope, realized that the car was not aquatic so changed into a low gear and attacked the hill. We fairly shot up as if we were surfacing from a depth charge attack. Turning at the top we were faced by a T junction.

'Which way, Jack? Port or starboard?' enquired Jim.

I could see our destination hard-a-port so Jim adjusted the helm and we moored on a piece of waste ground in front of Harnham Hall. Out of the car I removed my shoe and commenced cleansing operations again. I hoped that our host would not notice that my socks were of varying colours!

Kate

John Wake was there to greet us. He is one of the most unforgettable men I have ever had the privilege of meeting. Short of stature, wiry of frame, he had weathered well over eighty years in this beautiful but exposed place. His eyes twinkled, his humour was dry while a smile played genuinely about his mouth. His Northumbrian burr was pleasing and congruous.

I stood on the lofty crag on which the hall was built in 1415 by Swinburne. To the west I could see the rolling hills and alternating moors stretching towards the far distant Solway; Scotland beckoned from the north; Belsay seemed to be smothered in a basin to the south and the east hid the coast. The panoramic expanse was breathtaking and entrancing.

'Come in,' invited John as he led the way.

The main door was open to reveal a cheerful, pleasant and colourful hallway.

'This is a nail head door,' instructed John, 'which I reckon dates from 1415 but others put it into the sixteenth century.'

It was low and narrow and could have been easily defended in more troublesome times. We entered John's drawing room. 'This was the dining room in Kate's time,' began John.

'What a superb fireplace,' I remarked.

'In her day it had a huge beacon fire,' replied John.

'What's a beacon fire?' asked Jim who thought of beacons as being flares on hilltops.

'It was rather large like a blacksmith's with a huge cowl and had fitted bellows,' demonstrated John with his arms stretching to the size.

Just then I looked up and was amazed. A large, decorative circle of plaster, roughly seven feet in diameter dominated the ceiling. Inside the circle was a plaster sculpture of a dragon's head and shoulders. It was beautifully executed. The dragon's scales stood out in such clear relief as to appear almost real. John saw my uplifted gaze.

'That dragon predates Kate who died in 1670. See its shattered eye? I'll tell you about that later.'

He led the way to the staircase. It is the original construction and is in three short flights. The tower, dating from 1415, leads off the first landing and entering it we stepped back five hundred years to a time of elegance and grandeur interlocked with intrigue, vengeance, hatred and killing. The morning light dispelled the shadows and all thoughts of darkness and imprisonment. The square room was attractive; the walls stout and solid and the ceiling high and light. On one wall hung the family quarterings containing the arms of the Haselriggs and bearing the motto, _'Fey est tout'_.

'Ah, Faith is all,' I loosely translated and was immediately accepted as an academic by Jim.

A small bed lay alongside the north wall, a pleasant carpet softened our step and a chair and small table completed the furnishings. Two windows had originally given light but one, above the bed, is now sealed with impregnable stonework. The other window, looking towards the east, was open and revealed a breathtaking view. My eyes scanned the fields, moors and copses.

'See that gap in the trees half a mile away? It's called Pons' Gap,' said John.

'Why Pons? Should it be ponds, for Bolam lake is in that direction,' I asked.

'Bolam lake wasn't there in Kate's time. No. It is Pons. Pons and his man kept watch there. In the troublous times when the Scots and English were at each other's throats Pons and his man had the responsibility of warning the occupants of the hall of any impending danger or attack. Even in later days watch was kept there as the Border raiders and reivers followed the old highway from Scots Gap to Carter Bar. On modern ordnance maps the road is named as The Devil's Causeway. Frequently the hall was attacked but its stoutness and defensive position high on this crag prevented it from submission or destruction. There is a legend that during one attack a defender shot a single arrow from this window and impaled three men on the one arrow!'

'Now, John, tell me why this other window is walled up,' I requested.

Jim must have realized that a history lesson was about to

begin so he sat down on the bed. My sock clung to my right ankle like a plaster cast.

'To keep Kate in,' was the simple reply of John.

'Keep her in? Then why didn't they block up both windows? This open one is low and easy to reach even with the encumbrance of full skirts. She could have escaped through that,' I protested.

'Lean out of it; but not too far,' warned John.

'It looks east. It opens outward and there are no bars. Seems easy to me,' I said.

'Well; go on, stick your head out. Would you jump out of that window?' John asked.

There was a sheer drop of well over two hundred feet. It looked as if the tower had grown naturally from the heights of the crag.

'In Kate's day there was a moat at the bottom and a high defensive wall. See the trees? They are tall yet the tops of them do not come within a hundred feet of this window and even they were not here then.'

Then came my inevitable question.

'What was Kate doing here? Was she imprisoned in her own tower and home?'

'It's a long story, so let's go some place more comfortable,' suggested John.

'No. Do you mind if we stay here for the story. I feel somehow that Kate is here and I want the atmosphere.'

'She is here,' emphasized John as he began the sad tale of Catherine Babington. 'Kate's father was Sir Arthur Haselrigg, governor of Tynemouth. She was of outstanding beauty and once when in Durham City went into a public eating house to eat a pork pie.'

'I know about that, John, but I didn't know that it was a pork pie,' I laughed.

'A marriage for her to Colonel George Fenwick was arranged while she was still a young girl in order to cement better relations between the two families. The colonel was very much older than she was and he died soon after the marriage and she left Brinkburn.'

'That was an early tragedy for her,' I remarked.

'Not really,' rejoined John, 'for she was now free to marry the man she deeply loved; Major Philip Babington of Harnham Hall and Governor of Berwick.'

'She must have been a pretty bride in a pretty place,' I mused.

'Pretty without doubt but also a lady with a purpose,' said John, 'she and her husband were staunch Puritans in full sympathy with and support for the Covenanters.'

John paused then sat down on the small chair while I

pensively continued to look through the open window.

'During the Long Parliament,' continued John, 'Kate engaged her blacksmith, a huge man who could lift his anvil above his head and hurl it twenty five feet, to remove, by force, the vicar of Bolam from his pulpit and escort him beyond the parish boundaries. The vicar, the Reverend Foster, was a mean man who harboured far from Christian grudges and swore revenge. Philip and his wife installed a well known Covenanter, Mr Veitch as their minister. Kate had a small chapel of worship constructed in the garden of the hall. We'll see the remains of it later,' promised John.

'Stirring times and dedication to principles,' I remarked.

'All was peaceful and well ordered for a few years until the Restoration of the monarchy which eventually saw the reinstatement of Foster as Vicar of Bolam.'

'That would put the prelate among the pigeons,' I suggested.

'Oh, Foster was a wicked man,' was John's estimate of the cleric's character. 'This vengeful and determined man exercised his extensive power and sought to apprehend first the blacksmith, then Mr Veitch and of course the Lady Catherine.'

'Did he have such power?' I asked.

'He probably exceeded it,' said John, 'but he had influential supporters. What happened to the blacksmith has never been discovered. He disappeared from his smithy one day and was never seen again. Some said that he had fled but others hinted that he had met a violent death at the hands of the vicar's assassins. Mr Veitch was worshipping in the little chapel when assailants burst in and sought to kill him. He escaped through a very small door set high in the chapel wall. In later years this irrepressible evangelist was arrested while proclaiming the Word at Middleton. Imprisoned for a little while, he was eventually fined four cattle and two horses!'

'But what of Kate?' I enquired.

'She was less fortunate. Foster's men harrassed her for months with threats and actual bodily harm until finally the vicar had her imprisoned in her own tower.'

'How could that happen?' I was incredulous.

'All I know is that it did happen and that the unfortunate lady was incarcerated here for two years,' said John quietly, 'and it cost her life, for after two years of severe restriction she died in this room in 1670 at the age of thirty-six.'

I felt saddened. So many questions tortured my mind. Where was her husband? What powers did the vicar have? Who brought Kate sustenance? What exercise did she get? Was she ever allowed out of the narrow confines of her prison?

I didn't ask the questions but followed John and Jim from the tower and descended to the kitchen. A heartening glow spread its warmth from a Triplex range and the kettle sang an invitation from the firebar. The room was friendly and bright but still had the atmosphere of a prison. Heavy bars straddled the main window and the walls were at least three feet thick.

'In Kate's day,' began John, as if that time was the pinnacle of history, 'there was a large fire here too; not a beacon fire but an open fireplace behind which one could sit. There was of course a spit and also to one side, an oven-like bakery.'

'Why the thick bars on that window? Was this place also fortified against the possibility of Kate's intrusion?' I asked.

'No. These bars were to keep Scottish prisoners in. Ever since the place was built and for many years the Scots made many incursions into these parts and a ready but voluntary force of men were always at hand to resist. Prisoners were brought here and often used in exchange for English prisoners. Look over there, Did you ever see such a splendid bullseye window?' asked John.

It is indeed a magnificent window approximately eighteen inches in diameter and the glass must be between three and four inches thick. Despite this it is also heavily barred.

We walked into the drawing room again. The dragon's head fascinated me.

'I have something here I treasure most among all my

mementoes of Kate,' said John.

He went to a tall cabinet of solid mahogany, the lower section being a writing unit. The drawer opened easily and from it John took a silver frame containing a portion of window pane. The cabinet was antique and so was the glass, for it had clouded somewhat but the writing upon it was still clearly discernible. Handling it with extreme care and a great deal of affection he said to me, 'Kate wrote this in the tower only three months before she died.'

I took it reverently into my hands and read;

June 1670.   Philip Babington.

C. Babington.

How vain is the help of man.

K. Babington.

All is vanity. (This last line in Latin)

I wondered; was her husband also a prisoner with her? Was she losing hope? Was her husband free but seeking desperately to secure her freedom? How vain is the help of man? What help and was it men in general? So many unanswered questions but because they are unanswered they testify to the veracity of the story.

Jim followed me, in the wake of John Wake, to the garden outside. We veered right to a small gate marked 'Private'. Passing through this John led us down a narrow, dangerous stone stairway. It led to a turfed terrace. As we walked we passed the ruins of Kate's little chapel.

'Mr Veitch escaped through that door,' indicated John.

'Door?' I queried. 'You mean window.'

'No. It was a secret door.'

Its base was about three feet above ground level and it is about two feet high and eighteen inches wide. It is now blocked up with stonework.

'Foster's men searched for him not knowing that he was actually beneath their feet in a small crypt. As night fell the cottagers rescued him and cared for him for weeks without the knowledge of his pursuers,' related John.

Quietly we approached Kate's last resting place. Here was peace not turbulence; love not fear; Heaven not Hell.

Paradise had kissed this blessed plot in honour to a martyr of her faith; a lady whose radiant soul and invincible faith and courage could not be dimmed by months of incarceration. I sensed the sanctity of this unconsecrated ground as I approached it. What man in his presumption would not perform I am sure that God did.

It is not a burial site but a sepulchre hewn out of the solid crag. Fittingly no door held the homage of the seasons at bay. In winter the hoar frost would ensilver the darkness inside; springtime could waft the incense of blossom towards it; summertime would make the sepulchre golden at sunsets and the autumn confetti it with russet leaves which in turn provided a blanket against the harshness of Northumbrian winters. It is a fitting resting place for a lady who added not only her beauty but her grace to the fairness of nature. As the whole of nature breathes hope so does the precinct of this sacred place; yet here it is a stern, silent but eloquent rebuke to those who lacked Christian forgiveness and love. The Reverend Foster's remains may lie in a churchyard amid the myrtle boughs but where is his soul?

Having caused Kate to be held in a darkened tower for so long where the only true light was her sweet and forgiving personality he steadfastly refused to allow her a Christian burial in consecrated ground. For ten whole days her body lay on the surface until finally she was laid in this unconsecrated but heavenly blessed sepulchre.

Years later itinerant faws or tinkers stole her coffin for its lead content and her remains lay discarded on the cold, stone ground. Nature did its best to cover her until John Wake, Saintly John, recovered what was left of her and constructed a coffin which now lies where the original casket was laid. Above the coffin lies the ancient inscription;

> Here lies the body of Madam Babington who was laid in this sepulchre 9th September, 1690.

Kate's parents had brought the young girl up as a Christian and had set the foundation of her Puritan persuasion by their own adherence to Reformation principles. They were troublous times in every respect, politically and religiously. In the Church, high churchmen and low churchmen were continually in bitter conflict and the 1662 Book of Common Prayer did much to stabilize the position. Kate was well educated but her religious beliefs dominated her whole outlook. During her prolonged imprisonment in the tower she wrote a poem when she had probably realized that there would be no release for her except death. This sad little rhyme is now preserved on a board hung near to her remains in the sepulchre.

'In hopes of future bliss contented here I lie;
though I would have been pleased to live
yet was not displeased to die.
For life has its comforts and sorrows too
for which to the Lord of Heaven our thanks are due.
If it was otherwise our hopes here would rest
where nature tells us we cannot be blessed.
How far my hopes are vain or faulted well
God only knows; the last day will tell.'

I stood in silent homage to this amazing lady until John suggested that we return to the house. The sun had gained in height and warmth and again nature seemed to endorse my thoughts on Kate by its sheer joy and beauty. We walked between the trees to the outside of the tower and the hopeless grimness of Kate's imprisonment was evident in the steepness of the crag and the outside view of the stoned-up window.

Returning through the nail head door John led us to the kitchen door.

'See those pellet holes?' he asked. 'A previous owner of the hall claimed that Kate's spirit nightly perambulated between the tower and the kitchen. Deciding that enough was enough he decided to shoot the spectre. Loading his twelve bore he sat in wait facing the kitchen. Whatever it was he saw he blasted at it and peppered the lintel.'

'Did he then have any success in his slaughter of the after-life?' I enquired.

'Well, draw your own conclusions. The next night he was

so frustrated that he went into Kate's dining room and had a shot at the dragon. That is why it has no eye today,' said John.

'Do you think that he really was troubled by Kate's ghost?' I asked.

'Could have been,' mused John, 'on the other hand he was a well known alcoholic. In my opinion he was shooting at green snakes or pink elephants. The vicar rebuked his gross intemperance and he promised to reform. However, one afternoon the vicar saw him staggering from the inn carrying a jug full of ale.

' "You disappoint me, William. You promised to give up the demon drink," said the vicar, "and here you are with a brimming jug of the same."

' "Ah," was the reply, "I'm taking half a jug to my brother."

' "Half a jug; but that jug is full."

' "Yes, I'll have to drink the top half before I can get to my brother's half," said old William.

'So I reckon that this incurable soak saw more than Kate's ghost in the hall,' concluded John.

'Now, John, for a straight answer. Have you ever seen Kate's ghost?' I demanded.

John paused awhile. He looked up the stairs towards the tower. His eyes moved from there to the kitchen door. He seemed reluctant to speak. It was obvious that he loved Kate and was perhaps in her confidence.

'Have you ever seen the wind?'

'No.'

'But you know that it is there. Let's leave it at that.'

Evening Call

I was on my way to my daughter's home when the pale yellow strip of light warned me that I was low in spirit – the liquid kind – so I turned into my regular garage for replenishment. Bill, the owner, was at hand to see that the spirit did not overflow and that my credit was good. He replaced the petrol cap and led the way to his cash register past racks of newspapers, bagged potatoes and offers of free gifts. He checked my money, proffered me gift tokens and leaned across the counter confidentially.

'I understand that you are interested in ghost stories; that is true ones,' he said.

I was delighted. I was in no hurry. British Summer Time had commenced the previous weekend and the daylight would probably last until half past eight.

'Yes. Is yours true?' I asked.

'It actually happened to me, or should I say that I saw it,' he whispered as another customer appeared. The man paid for his fuel and lingered over his choice of brand of cigarettes arousing in me my latent impatience. He left. Bill continued.

Jack in the Spirit

'A year ago this month I went with three friends to climb in the Lake District. We did not intend to do any rough climbing, like scaling crags or rock faces, leaving that to the experts which we were certainly not. We kept strictly to the ridges and they were steep enough. Our object was Helvellyn. One of my companions is an accountant and the other a garage owner like myself.'

Business was booming. Customers queued up behind me. Bill had to break off from telling his story. I prayed that his business would suffer a temporary recession for an hour.

'Hello,' said one of the customers to me, 'What are you doing here? I thought that your car ran on faith.'

'It is moved by the spirit,' I retorted.

At last my prayer was answered and Bill's takings dropped. He resumed his story.

'The going was slow. We had set off from Patterdale but my heart almost failed on Striding Edge. Ever been on it? There's foot room only and it falls sheer away. When I looked up and saw the snow line perilously near I was for turning back but the others had more guts and I wouldn't admit to being chicken.

'Wisely we were all wearing the correct clothing and had adequate equipment. No one should attempt that climb, even in the summer, unless they are properly fitted out with the advised gear. At times we sank knee deep in the snow. Breathless but triumphant we reached the summit.'

Bill must have thought that I was a climber for he remarked, 'You know how it is, Jack, when you get to the top. You stand and look around and below at the panorama of hills and dales. It makes the climb well worthwhile. The three of us stood looking through the clear air at the Lake District spread out before us like a contoured map. It was exhilarating.'

He described the view to me and then said dramatically:

'Suddenly there were four of us.'

'Four? Where did the other come from?' I asked.

'Don't know. He was just there,' Bill stated, 'I saw him

as plainly as I can see you. He was dressed in the climbing outfit favoured in the thirties and I saw his short coat actually blowing in the breeze. He stood looking around, then he looked at us and smiled. It was a happy smile and immediately he seemed to be out of breath or certainly distressed in his breathing. He was young and clean

shaven. I was about to ask him if he felt alright when he began the descent. He moved slowly and uncertainly and I felt that we ought to invite him to accompany us, when at a distance of no more that twenty yards he literally and definitely vanished! He had made tracks in the snow and they suddenly ceased. There was no place for him to fall over or into. He just disappeared as quickly as he had appeared at the first place!'

'And then what?' I asked.

'Well, nothing really. That was it. We all were startled and thought that he was a harbinger of disaster but he wasn't. We all got down safely. Our hotel manager at Patterdale told us that the apparition was seen frequently up there.'

Three customers came into the garage. I counted them carefully and left!

I reached Christine's house. The walls of the sixteenth century manor house looked mellow in the twilight. Shadows were gathering among the graves in the adjacent churchyard and the rooks cawed as they built their ragged nests in the bellcote of the church. It was very cold and the lights of evening were beginning to shine in the distant village across the fields. I saw the vet's car alongside the front door and parked mine beside his. Christine answered the door to my bell ring.

'Lovely to see you. Ian is almost finished. He's in the kitchen. He's been inoculating Flurry and has examined Chableigh and Mindy.'

Evidently he was finished his veterinary operations for the three labradors came bounding towards me. Ian was washing his hands at the kitchen sink.

'Hello, Jack. Nice to see you. Christine has just invited me to have a sherry.'

'Then she can pour one for me,' I said hopefully as I led the way into the drawing room. It is a large room befitting a manor house. A log fire crackled merrily and the dogs settled in the window seats. Christine loves all animals. A lithograph of a bull's face adorned one wall, a whale thrashed the sea with its massive tail in oils near to the door, two highland scenes depicting kylies hung on either side of the fireplace and Paul's excellent poem 'Swans' was framed and hanging prominently.

I sank into an easy chair and Ian sat near to the fire. Christine poured the sherry.

'How's that dog of yours getting on? Did the injections I gave him to dampen his love ardour work?' asked Ian.

'Ruff. No. He's as keen as ever and has ideas above his station for he's been hanging around the viscount's kennels. But I must tell you a story I heard at the garage on my way here,' I said.

I related the tale of the Helvellyn foursome.

'We have ghosts at home,' volunteered Ian the vet.

He lives not very far from my cottage.

'Friendly or otherwise?' I enquired.

'Both. Some wraith passes through the house leaving a most fragrant scent behind her. It really is most pleasant but she is invisible.'

'Would you like me to exorcise her?' I offered.

'No, not her; I'd rather you'd exorcise my wife,' replied Ian lightheartedly.

'You said ghosts. Are there others?' I asked.

'Yes. Horses,' answered Ian.

'Not the four horses of the Apocalypse?' I quipped.

'You know my house, Jack. It has a cobbled courtyard. Fiona, who you christened, is more than interested in horses. She spends all her spare time with them.'

'Maybe the interest will fade when she gets a young man,' I suggested.

'Oh, no. She's got both right now. The other evening, in fact the Sunday on which the clocks were put forward, I had just settled in my chair when I heard horses in the courtyard.

' "Fiona; your wretched horses are loose. You must have left the field gate open. I've warned you about that before. Now go out and put them where they belong". Fiona was stretched out reading a teenager magazine and obviously resented any disturbance.

' "If anyone left that gate open it wasn't me," grumbled the girl.

' "Never mind who it was," I rebuked. "Go out and deal with them before they do any damage" I instructed her.

'She still hesitated. I was anxious in case they got into my garden. I had that very afternoon planted a magnolia tree and I did not want it trampled.

' "Come on, Fiona. Get yourself off the rug and stir yourself. You can hear them can't you?"

' "Yes", persisted Fiona, "but one of them's yours".

' "Listen, lass; go out to them and don't argue" I commanded.

'She went, reluctantly. The noise of hooves upon the cobbles ceased and Fiona shouted, "Dad; come here."

'I went out. The field gate was securely fastened and chained and our horses were at the far side of the field grazing quietly.

' "They weren't our horses, Dad, and the gate is still fastened."

' "Bit of a mystery that. I wonder whose horses they are," I pondered. No one living near to us has horses. I walked around the place and could see no sign of other horses anywhere.

'I've heard them twice since then. I don't know how many there are because the noise always ceases when I go to the courtyard. Maybe you would like to come up some evening in the hope that you might hear them,' invited Ian.

The firelight now warmed the room with a heartening glow while the light outside slowly yielded to the night. Chableigh lay on one window seat at the end of the room.

'That window used to be the main door into this manor house before alterations were carried out fairly recently. I'm sure that our resident ghost still uses it as a door,' said Christine.

'I didn't know you had one here,' I remarked.

'Oh, yes,' Christine replied, 'It's like Ian's. It's a lady for sure. Often I scent a fragrance as it wafts past me from that window, across the room and out towards the music room.'

'Another fragrant lady,' I exclaimed.

'Yes, and I don't want her exorcised. I feel that she is good. We've called her Margery,' informed Christine.

'Why Margery?' asked Ian.

'She was known as the Lady of Ulgham,' replied Christine, 'and she lived almost the whole of the thirteenth century. She was twice widowed. She was generous to her tenants at Ulgham and regarded not only with respect but with real affection. She truly cared about people and was deeply religious. I'm sure that there was a church here in Saxon times. Dad, your friend who doused Mitford church with divining rods did so here and found what he claimed to be Saxon foundations. Margery no doubt gave generously to the church and to the religious order or itinerant monks from Lindisfarne who served it. I think that she must have been a lovely lady and she's welcome here in what was at one time her own home.'

The vet gave the dogs a friendly pat, looked at Christine's stuffed birds and realizing that they were beyond any treatment he could give them, bade us all a hearty goodnight.

I stayed. My grandchildren were more interested in naval stories and I had to listen to accounts of their play on the rugby field. Both Simon and Alastair played for the local 'minis'. Naomi, not to be outdone, thrilled me with terrifying stories of how she wielded her hockey stick in such an abandoned fashion that she might have added a few opponents to the spirit world. It was still the Easter holidays so they were a little later than usual in going to bed.

'I'll have to go soon,' I said, 'It's quite dark now, but before I go, seeing as Ian got us talking about animal spirits, did you ever hear of Chris' dog?'

'Yes; I can vaguely remember something about it. Tell me again,' requested Christine.

Chris is my twin sister. She lived on a farm which had previously been a monastery dedicated to St. Stephen. Henry VIII's attentions ended its monastic functions and the buildings became barns and implement sheds. The house in which Chris was living had been the chapel. Over the main doorway was an archway which was inscribed in Latin, 'Glory to God and his sacred name.' Many religious carvings were built into the walls. The main east end window of the chapel now served both the dining room and the bedroom, reaching the floor in the bedroom and the ceiling in the dining room. My mother swore that she saw odd manifestations and at one time heard an organ playing while she was staying there. There were several rumours of hooded monks who still appeared among the buildings. I never saw anything but Chris did.

Her husband, Alf, was due to come in from the fields for his lunch. A cheerful fire burned in the dining room grate. Chris entered to prepare the table for the meal. To her astonishment she saw a huge mastiff lying on the hearth-rug. It was a magnificent creature and looked very friendly. Chris never feared any animal but she was anxious that if Nell and Jess, Alf's two collies, came in they might attack the dog. Collies are notoriously jealous dogs. Chris knelt beside the mastiff and stroked it. She took hold of the heavy, studded collar to see if it bore an owner's name. As she did so the dog vanished!

The Turn of the Tide

It was a waxing moon that shattered itself into millions of dancing diamonds upon the surface of a slumbering sea which was reserving energy for its regular retreat from its appointed bounds. The pale light bathed the coast in uncertain shadows which were both mysterious and frightening. A halyard flapped against a flag pole with irritating monotony sometimes startling as it gave an extra heavy lash.

In the lee of the sheltered wall at the shoreward end of the pier, oblivious to darkness and light and engrossed only in the light of love, Kathleen and Ian embraced. Although it was midnight, time did not exist for them as they looked into the eternal, other-worldly realm of love that lay, a placid sea, deep in their eyes. A cloud darkened the scene. Berwick upon Tweed lost its demarcations and only a gentle sighing betrayed the sea. Kathleen sighed too before her lips surrendered to the warm, eager kisses of Ian. She lowered her eyelids lest anything should intrude into her star-spangled heaven. Her sojourn in Paradise lasted an age yet seemed to be over in a twinkling. She kept her eyes closed as Ian whispered tenderly of his love for her. His lips again sought hers and Paradise was regained.

As the cloud moved on restoring the seascape, the long finger of the pier, bent at its knuckle, lay luminous and spectral snaking out to its protective nail, the beacon which fitfully and silently stabbed into the darkness. Kathleen, nestled in the unrelenting embrace of her lover, opened her eyes. A limited mist dimmed the immediate foreground. Beyond it and about it the sea murmured in its sleep and the distant lights of Tweedmouth lost their sharpness. Silently and definitely the mist formed itself into a figure. She could clearly discern a presence prying into those blissful moments which were their's by right of love and their's alone.

Hoping that she could eradicate a third and unwelcome party she closed her eyes tightly. Ian raised his hand to caress her hair and she opened her eyes intending to reward his hand with a kiss. Now there was no doubt that a nocturnal observer had joined them.

She was not of this world! She stood, silently, pathetically concentrating her gaze upon them as if with intense yearning. Her long, white robe fluttered gently although there was no breeze. She emanated an aura of unsettled wistfulness which was gentle rather than terrifying. This pitiful figure seemed to reach out to Kathleen's heart and understanding as if she had some problem of unrequited love or betrayal or a sadness and searching for her lover who never returned. Kathleen experienced an affinity with

this visitor from beyond the grave. She felt an urge to help but knew not how. The spirit seemed to draw her into a ghostly embrace and now Kathleen began to fear and clung almost desperately to Ian, for she felt that if she took the unearthly visitor into her arms she would never return to this life but would tread a ghostly trail into realms unknown. She felt all this in a very real way. The tugging of the phantom at her inner self was no imagination.

Fearing that this apparition had come to take her she

sought the security of her lover.

'Ian, look very carefully and slowly behind you,' she whispered.

'What for?' His answer was barely audible.

'Just look,' asked Kathleen.

He turned. He saw. He was shocked.

'Let's go; come on; quickly,' he began as his legs indicated his intention.

'One moment,' requested the girl.

She felt that she wanted to flee away but somehow, inexplicably, she was drawn to this ethereal presence and deep within her inner soul Kathleen formed the invitation.

'Come and tell me.'

The woman in white now seemed to glow in a warmth that is unfamiliar among the denizens of beyond.

Ian hesitated and looked, unable to understand or respond.

'Come, Kathleen, come.' His shout echoed beyond the time and distances of this world. He reached out and snatched Kathleen's hand and the White Lady was there no more.

Kathleen told me of her experience as I stood at the counter in the bank which employed her.

'It's true, Mr Richardson. I saw it. Ian saw it. It only happened last week. I'll never forget it. I've been waiting to tell you. Oh, please believe me. It did happen,' she pleaded.

Picking up my pittance of a pension I asked her,

'Would it be the spirit of the woman who for over twenty years hung from the sea bastions in a wicker basket?'

'I don't know; I've never heard of her,' she replied.

'If she was young and lovelorn I don't suppose it could have been that woman. Have you heard of the Grey Lady of Berwick's Walls?'

'Yes I have but this ghost was white,' Kathleen replied.

'Tell me, Kathy, had you ever been on the pier at midnight before this,' I asked.

She lowered her eyes, hesitated and then admitted, 'It's a favourite spot of ours.'

'Did you ever see anything supernatural or even unusual before that night?'

'No.' Her answer was simple and honest.

'Do you think that it could have been a trick of the light?' I suggested.

'Even if it had been it could not account for the strong, almost magnetic, feeling that drew me towards the woman," offered Kathy.

'Have you been back?' I continued.

'Yes; once.'

'Aren't you afraid?' I asked her.

'No, not with Ian beside me. In fact I went because I half hoped that I would see the woman again. I'll not really be happy until I see her again. Somehow I feel that she needs me. I'm sure that she is not appearing for any evil purpose and that her visitation is not a warning,' explained Kathleen.

'If you see her again tell her that you understand and want to help her, but make sure that Ian is with you. I don't want my favourite cashier to be counting heavenly treasures before her time,' I advised.

A young lady tugging at a child who incessantly sucked at a stick of barley sugar came into the bank, invested her child allowance, glanced at me well-wrapped for a winter's day, then propelled the gummed-up infant to the biting wind outside. I thought that while this arctic weather continued it was unlikely that Kathleen and Ian would be cuddling on the pier. The back seats of the Playhouse would be warmer and the only ghost they would be likely to encounter would be *The Phantom of the Opera*.

I sought to give Kathy an explanation.

'Have you heard of Bobby Shafto?'

'Of course. "Bobby Shafto went to sea," ' Kathy responded.

'Well perhaps we have a parallel in your story. It wasn't the Grey Lady and it doesn't relate to any of the stories about Mary, Queen of Scots. It could be a girl whose sailor lover went to sea never to return. Maybe his ship foundered

46

but I think it more likely that he deserted her. The wind would fill his sails and blow both him and his fancies away.'

'Why not shipwreck?' asked Kathleen.

'Because if he had loved her truly then I think they would not be reunited in the spiritual sphere, whereas according to you, she is still searching,' I said.

There was an influx of clients into the bank. A prosperous looking matron carrying a handbag as big as a kitbag took up station behind me and she emanated an aura of impatience and importance. She would brook no delay. So our conversation was concluded.

I go to the bank again next month. Will I hear of peace or the continuing saga of an endless search?

Over and Out

The dogfights of 1940 above our southern skies had resounded again intermingled with the dogmatics of a naval sky-pilot. I zoomed like a spitfire towards the heavenly altitudes and thundered like a hurricane to shoot down the deadly flights of evil. Beelzebub and the swastika were shot down in an aerial onslaught of Biblical texts.

I fought this battle from the dizzy heights of the pulpit in South Gosforth Church, on Battle of Britain Sunday. Tired out by the aerobatic gyrations of my delivery, I drove homewards. Darkness had closed in with a vengeance shrouding its blanket with mist and rain. Now and then a signpost materialized, slipping by like wraiths fingering from and to the unknown and hidden. Cats-eyes glistened from the ground like imploring souls warning from their ghastly imprisonment. The mist swirled ghost-like and ethereal before my dipped headlights and the world seemed to be wrapped in mystery.

Then it was I saw it. A body. It lay grotesquely across the middle of the road like a dead limb from a dying tree. I parked my car broadside on to any traffic that might err in that direction although the road was at that hour deserted. I left my headlights blazing. I bent over my grim discovery. His head was flattened as if by a road-roller, leaving one eye stranded at the base of his nose though still connected by a sliver of membrane. I felt sick as I saw the grey mess I thought could only be his brains.

I ran in search of a phone box. I broke the four-minute-mile when I reached an inn called The Kicking Cuddy. From there I phoned the police.

'Go back and wait for our arrival. Don't move him,' they ordered.

I ran. The pain hit me.

'Queer place to get the stitch,' I thought as my chest hurt like Hell as if a cuddy had kicked it.

Thankfully I crept into my bed. Ethel, my wife, was already asleep in the other twin bed. At a quarter to two an excrutiating pain threw me out of the bed.

I crawled about the floor breathless and beating the deck in utter agony. I could not cry out. Eventually I managed to reach the bedside and kneel there panting and painful. I did not wish to disturb Ethel who was still asleep. After an age I levered myself into the bed and found considerable ease sitting upright. As the pain decreased I lay flat. Almost at once I was in untold agony. I gasped and could breath no more. The pain had hit me like a thunderbolt, but it was drastic yet momentary.

Suddenly I was at ease; no pain; no breathlessness, in fact no breath. I sat up. My body didn't. I looked at my body lying still and flat. I was leaving my body as if discarding a pair of wellington boots. I felt warm and comfortable and reassured. There was no panic.

'This is it,' I thought.

I felt about half way out of my earthly shell when I willed myself back to life. I could actually feel myself going back and there was no doubting the severity of the pain which hit me on re-entry. I cried out. Ethel heard me, and cared for me as I'm sure the heavenly angels had been preparing to

48

minister to me. I lay flat in a narrow, hard bed in the infirmary. I was to be there for six weeks.

'You've punctured your heart,' informed the specialist, 'and on paper you were a dead man.'

'Never mind the theory, doc; I did die,' I replied as I told him of my experience of partial elevation. He listened intently and told me that he had heard from several patients of similar happenings.

I went to Inveraray to convalesce. Kirsty, who eventually died within two weeks of her hundredth birthday, mothered me. She kept the Temperance Hotel in the lovely highland town and it was the best house in which to get a wee dram. The old, stone staircase was spiral and often bemused even Kirsty after a few drams. It broke step on the first landing to lead to Kirsty's private sitting room on the right which overlooked the loch and pierhead. My bedroom was directly opposite and was as irregular as the staircase. Electric blankets were unknown there and two large stone bottles were my constant companions in my bed. The house was over two hundred and fifty years old and Kirsty maintained that there were several unpaying guests from bygone ages.

Remembrance Sunday saw the minister beleaguered up the glens and unable to reach his parish so the elders asked me to conduct the service of remembrance, first in the kirk and then at the war memorial which stood sentinel by the lochside. As I walked beside the solitary piper, memories flooded back to me. As the dirge 'Flowers of the Forest' tugged at my heartstrings so the ghosts of past acquaintances lived again. I seemed to walk with my old shipmate Malcolm who had been mercilessly massacred by a German fighter pilot while drifting helplessly in a life raft. I saw the form of old Bob Rose, with whom I was billetted, and long since dead, standing at his door. I heard again the bustle and rattle of Combined Operations although the air was still and silent. I felt sad yet also at one with those with whom I served.

The wreaths had been laid; the bugle call had echoed up

the glens and the kilted had paid their homage. I sat with Kirsty relaxing after lunch. Her fire glowed brighter as the winter sky grew darker.

'There's snow up the glens. We'll have it before the day is out,' she forecast. I told her of my sad thoughts and in a way shared them with her for she knew all the naval lads who had passed through Inveraray. We reminisced with true and deep feeling.

'I can tell you of a real ghost here,' she said.

'At Inveraray?' I asked.

'Well, actually on the loch,' she seemed to reflect.

'Tell me, Kirsty, I'm really interested,' I pleaded.

'Only the older folk of Inveraray know of it. I doubt if incomers know it,' she remarked. 'Incomers' were those who were not born there even though they may have resided there for fifty years.

The afternoon's gloom deepened towards an early darkness as the first flakes of snow began to fall so gently and quietly. Up in Glen Shira, Mima's grave was taking on a white mantle while Bob Rose, her brother-in-law, had a dry-stone wall to shelter his narrow bed of which he was the permanent tenant.

'The legend relates that during the time of the plague,' began Kirsty, 'an old boatman from the head of the loch seemed to be immune from the deadly ravishes of the black disease. Dressed in an enveloping, black cloak over a dark tartan and wearing a black bonnet with streaming black ribbons he daily rowed the seven miles to collect the dead. Their bodies were laid on the shingle where they mend and dry the salmon nets today. No one would watch as he loaded his small boat with its grim cargo. Where the channel runs deep he committed the bodies to the waters. There is a whirlpool there and is easily seen from the road down to Cairndow and which is still known as The Pit.'

Kirsty informed me that half the population perished in the plague.

'When the scourge was over the old boatman was seen no more. No one knew what happened to him. His wee croft beside the loch remained deserted and fell into ruin. No one ever goes near the place nowadays.'

I sat back and contemplated the fire. The room had darkened now except for the occasional fitful flicker from the embers. Kirsty continued in a hushed tone.

'People began to report that on the eve of a death at Inveraray his ghostly figure was to be seen rowing the waters with muffled oars. The last report of him was when Sandy died two years ago.'

Kirsty had an odd-job man who was also a faithful friend. He was extremely pleasant, always courteous and had a good sense of humour. He claimed to be fey; to possess a second sense which was usually restricted to the seventh child of a seventh child. He and I were walking along the edge of the loch having walked over the hump-backed bridge by the castle when he said to me,

'What's that out there?'

He indicated the middle of the loch. I looked. The moon was full; the waters diamond crested. The hills behind St. Catherine's were white topped with their dusting of snow and clearly visible but I could not discern anything on the surface of the water.

'Something's there,' insisted Archie.

He peered in a concentrated manner as if to bring an object into focus.

'I still can't see anything,' I had to admit.

'It's the Black Boatman; look at his bonnet.'

Perhaps it was in my imagination but I thought that I saw a ripple on the calm water like a wake of a small boat but I did not see a boat or a boatman. Archie was transfixed. The moon went behind a snowcloud. All was dark again.

'It was him alright,' whispered Archie. Let's go and see if Kirsty is alright.'

Kirsty was in the spirit; whisky.

The following morning to my relief, and I'm sure to that of Archie too, we were still in the land of the living.

I returned home to my parochial duties as one returned from the dead. Archie, aged 44, died suddenly shortly afterwards.

Baleakin

We met outside the entrance to the Birks o' Aberfeldy. The sunshine was warm for May but the nights were still chilly and in the dark hours ghoulies, wierdies and howlies haunt the shadows of the Birks. Robert worked at the Crown Hotel but this was his day free of service to the Crown. At one time he had resembled a ghoulie with his untamed beard which had looked like a misplaced sporran. Now he was clean-shaven except for a bushy moustache which acted as a filter for strong Scottish ale, dregs and thick soup. It also had the effect of a word-processor for by the time his speech had struggled through its undergrowth the words became decipherable.

'What a surprise, Jack; what are you doing here in

Aberfeldy?' he enquired.

'I'm staying at Findynate and I'm looking for haggis,' I replied.

'Och; there's all sorts in the Birks but I've never seen a haggis in there,' he offered.

'No, Robert, I'm going to the butcher,' I said.

'The best one here is McGrouther's. The Crown gets all its meat from there. Haggis is their speciality. So is venison. I reckon that his lads sneak around Findynate at nights,' suggested Robert. 'I'm going up the road so I'll walk as far as the butcher's shop with you.'

We reached the shop. Robert's upper-lip fungus twitched like divining rods as he caught the scent of either a bonny highland lassie or the disinfectant from the chemist's shop which was opposite. Whatever it was he bade me goodbye and followed the trail.

The legend, 'Duncan McGrouther (Aberfeldy) Butcher, Bacon Curer and Game Dealer' adorned the premises. As this establishment is the purveyor of meat to the Crown I had expected to see 'By Appointment' above the doorway but that slogan appeared only alongside the portals of the doctors' surgery on the side of the crossroads. Difficult to distinguish among a shop full of customers was a pig's head. The absence of a body verified that they were indeed bacon curers. In the window stretched a line of haggis in regimental order, which was a contradiction of their carefree state in the wild.

'Yes sir?' queried Mr McGrouther as it became my turn to be served. He held a cutlass in his hand like the old chiefs of clans and his clan motto was emblazoned on his blue and white striped apron; FRAY BENTOS.

'May I have two haggis, please,' I supplicated.

The intellectual butcher looked pained.

'Haggi, sir, in the plural,' I was corrected.

'Aye then, twa haggi,' I responded.

My literary standard having been accepted, the butcher continued;

'Now, sir, would you be wanting male or female?'

Now, in death, the grey bodies of eight haggi were stretched along the counter as if upon a mortuary slab.

'I'll take one of each sex. Maybe I'll start a haggis farm. But tell me; are they fresh?' I asked.

The butcher looked pained.

'Fresh? Certainly. They were caught only this forenoon at Weem,' assured my wildlife expert.

'I do hope that you didn't use a gin-trap or any inhumane contraption,' I expressed vehemently, 'I'm a member of the R.S.P.C.A.'

'No, nothing like that. Nor did we shoot them. Pellets spoil the texture of the flesh.'

'Then how did you catch them? Poison gas?' I asked.

'The only way; catapult,' acclaimed the butcher, 'and it's a skilled sport because the only vulnerable spot is behind their right ear.'

Thus assured I bought two. As I was about to leave Mrs McGrouther with a disarming smile came from the backshop carrying two mini haggi.

'Look,' she said. 'Twins.'

This rather upset me as I am a twin.

Having purchased the requisites for the embalming of the haggi; neeps and whisky, I returned to Findynate.

'Ethel, I have a brace of haggi here, if they haven't nibbled their way out of the bag.'

'We'll eat them tomorrow,' Ethel said heartlessly, 'remember, we have to go out for a meal tonight.'

I placed my purchases carefully in a hutch apart from the whisky which was stowed in another container.

The evening came. Ethel carefully closed the door behind us, not out of consideration for the haggi, but because we had spotted two deer which were grazing at the edge of the trees. Their camouflaged hides were almost invisible to us but they heard our faint footsteps upon the grass and like fleeting spirits they vanished into an undergrowth of darkness. As we walked the vaulted aisle beneath the trees the songbirds rendered their evening hymn of praise and thanksgiving. Now and then a startled rabbit fled into the longer grass upon which the setting sun cast long shadows. The ubiquitous gnats danced their short minuet of life in clouded clusters and the collared doves cooed their lullabies to nature.

Tom and Jean had invited us to a clootie dumpling supper!

'Come awa' in,' said Tom, 'Sit yoursells doon. Now, Ethel, a wee dram? What aboot you, Jack? A drappie o' the hard stuff?'

We both settled for sherry.

Jean was in the kitchen supervising the last few minutes of the five hour preparation of the clootie dumpling. It is what I would describe as a utility food; it is the main evening meal; the portion remaining is fried up for breakfast and if any still remains then it is eaten as cake at teatime! We were snugly seated around the fireside and Jean supplied us with individual trays and plates and cutlery although I had expected either a cutlass or a harpoon. Then in she walked bearing the rival to the great chieftain of the pudding race, the clootie dumpling.

It looked like a road bollard which had been flattened by a steamroller! Jean had graced it with a single candle the flame of which smoked heavenward in hope or penitence or perhaps in supplication for those about to eat. Jean generously carved a huge wedge and deposited it upon my platter. It tasted delicious but the quantity was so great that I had to struggle to devour all of it.

'Ha'e some mair,' offered Jean.

'No, thank you. That was splendid and most satisfying,' I replied.

'Noo, look here. Aa went all the way to Perrrth for the ingredients especially for you. So come on; pass your plate.'

There was no denying her and soon another massive wedge obscured the thistle pattern on the plate, and once again I resumed my marathon mastication of multiple mouthfuls.

I felt that I could not rise from my chair afterwards, so as the darkness gathered outside, I sat and talked. I told them of my conversation with the butcher and received even more instruction from Tom on the wiles of the winsome haggis.

'Talking aboot the ghoulies of the Birks, the person you ought to meet is Alasdair,' recommended Tom.

'Why? Is he a ghoulie?' I asked, as I would not have been surprised at anything in that land of spirits.

'No,' laughed Tom, 'he lives in the most haunted house in Scotland. It's no far doon the road fra here. You should go tomorrow. Turn left on the main road for less than a mile, then take the first driveway on the left. Ye canna miss it,'

But I did! The noonday sun was fierce. My car windows were lowered to allow an intake of air but that was warm and sultry and failed to cool me. A bee buzzed into the car and then buzzed out. I found the entrance to the driveway by observing the lodge which looked bright and cheery and far removed from the darkness of unwelcome denizens of hades, but the driveway as such did not exist. It was overgrown by thistles and long grasses which at intervals effectively obscured numerous potholes. When my car wheels hit them I was jerked so violently that I felt sure that before I could reach Baleakin House I would have slipped innumerable discs.

Where was Baleakin House? I had followed the alleged track for three quarters of a mile up a rough gradient of about one in six to find further progress in the car impossible as a huge, five-barred gate straddled my blocked course. A chain and padlock, seemingly obtained from the dungeons of Stirling Castle, secured the gate to an iron stanchion which in turn was held to a stone wall by numerous foundry-made staples.

I left the car and climbed over the gate. A hill obscured the view so I climbed it in the hope of seeing my destination beyond it. I scoured the scenery with shaded eyes but the countless hills, which rose one after another in ever increasing altitude, topped out the sky without any signs of human habitation. I felt lost, desolate and bewildered. I reclimbed the gate to gain access to my car. I was about to climb into the front seat when I heard a voice!

It was thin, as if a cry caught in the reeds or the soulful whimper of a lost soul. I could see no soul either human or from the underworld. I leaned against my car. Had I imagined it? Perhaps it was the breeze in the thicket but this was not feasible as there was no breeze and no thicket. A little unnerved I actually sat in my car when the voice came again. This time it had a little more substance. I again vacated the car and looked with shaded eyes around me. Someone had definitely called. Was it a stray spectre from Baleakin or some mischievous sprite from the corries on the hills?

Eventually, turning fully into the glare of the sun, I saw a dwelling place. It was half-hut and half-caravan and it was only partially visible behind a bush. I walked towards it. Standing inside the half door was a man. He looked as old as Methuselah. His withered cheeks were tanned and his hair was held back by a bootlace. His ears seemed to be out of proportion and would have been more suited to an elephant and his neck was not like Annie Laurie's but rather like a dried leek. Despite his appearance he was most pleasant.

He smiled, revealing ancient, toothless gums and again the soft weak voice spoke.

'Are ye looking for a body?'

I thought that his choice of words could have have been bettered.

'There's nae body asides ma own self up here,' he continued.

'I am looking for someone or rather for a house,' I said, 'Baleakin House.'

'Och aye; but ye passed it doon the brae,' he said.

'I didn't see any house on the way up,' I protested.

'Mebbe not,' he replied, 'It's te the reet hand ye ken and the track's a wee bittie dense. I'll show ye the way. Turn ya vehicle aroond and I'll gan before ye.'

He guided my car reversals, as the track fell steeply away

on the one hand and a wicked ditch was a hazard on the other hand. Then the kindly old fossil began his walk in front of the car. It was almost a half mile down the road, or rather track, before he stopped.

'Alang there, and guidday to ye,' he wished me as he turned his back on the right hand track and with amazing dexterity hurried away as if wishing to avoid contact with the house of hauntings.

A centre ridge of earth and grasses scraped the underside of my car as I bumped along, as if on a choppy sea. Suddenly there was a clearing and the rubble heaped remains of a house. Like a gaunt, swollen finger, one section of a building defied the encroaching bracken and emphasized the scene of dereliction and ruin. I alighted from the car and looked around me. Stones that had once proudly carried the arms of a proud Scottish family now lay in discarded confusion among other relics of a noble edifice. A demolition team must have carried out their destruction speedily and departed when completed with equal haste. I looked across the pleasing vista of the valley to where the hills, beyond their tree-line, were intimate with the sky. The River Tay played hide and seek with the bushes along its banks and following the same course a road ribboned its way towards Ballinluig. Behind me the hills had a dark shadow which merged with desolation and even mystery. A large bird circled overhead; a buzzard no doubt, yet to my state of mind prevailing at that moment it became a vulture.

I hesitated, then walked slowly towards the existing building. It was square; defiantly square and stood like a grim tombstone marking change and decay. As I rounded the gable end I saw a man. He seemed to be so incongruous that I felt that he must be ethereal. He bent over a section of grass which had been rescued from the heather and gorse. He was surrounded by books. They stood or lay on the ground in multiple confusion.

'Good morning. Can I presume that you are Alasdair?' I greeted him.

'Aye; and ye?' he asked.

'Jack Richardson,' I replied, 'I'm staying at Findynate.'

'Aye; the lady there told me about you. You're a minister, aren't you?' he asked.

'Yes. What are you doing with all these books?' I asked.

'Sorting them out. It's a full time job; I have so many.'

He led me up a flight of six stone steps. We entered the kitchen. It was piled high with more books and a zig-zag way through them led past the washing-up sink to the living room. This too was a profusion of books.

'There's a chair in here somewhere,' began Alasdair, 'ah, here it is,' as he unearthed a wooden, upright chair from behind a mountain of tomes. He offered me the chair while he perched on a convenient stack of weighty books.

'I am a vegetarian and teetotaller. Can I offer you a glass of lemon juice?'

'Thank you,' I replied, 'I'd appreciate that.'

From behind yet more books he produced a bottle and soon discovered two mugs. As I sipped I asked, 'Where's the big house; Baleakin House?'

'Bulldozed to the ground,' replied Alasdair.

'Why?'

'Have ye no heard that it was the most haunted house in the whole of Scotland?' he asked.

'Until yesterday I had never heard of it, but was it so bad that demolition was the only remedy?' I commented.

'Bad. It was worse than that; it was devilish; it was evil; it was cursed,' the bookworm emphasized.

I thought that he was not going to give me any further information and was about to question him further but he guessed my intent and continued, 'There were so many ghosts and apparently a growing colony of them as if others beckoned the unsettled from their beds of clay, that knocking it down was the only answer.'

'Did they try exorcism?' my ritualistic self asked.

'Yes, over many years; in fact over a century at least, but it was all useless. A Roman priest lived here for months and even he had to leave helpless and afraid. All the powers he summoned were of none avail,' answered Alasdair.

'Were they so troublesome that they had to destroy a house?' was my next query.

'Troublesome? Aye. They were violent and they were not all human,' he surprised me.

'What do you mean? Non-human ghosts?'

'There were dogs and terrifying creatures. Doors were knocked down like paper by their ghostly strength. There were terrible hammerings on walls; screeches, apparitions; the lot,' catalogued Alasdair.

'Did they do any actual physical injury to the people living here? Were people hurt?'

'A guid few were injured but mair were terrified oot o' their wits. It is said that at least two people went mad and one committed suicide. Maybe he felt that if he could beat them he would join them. There was one they called the monster. He seemed able to inflate himself, or rather itself, to a towering ten feet in all directions and fill the place with not only darkness but a putrid smell of decaying flesh. No one can really describe the horror; not even those who experienced it,' my host informed me.

'How about dogs? You're suggesting that there is a hereafter for them too and that they too can become earthbound and haunt in such a ferocious manner,' I protested.

'There were dogs alright. Records tell of hounds and mongrels, of drooling jowls and snapping teeth. The worst offender seems to have been a massive, black dog who always accompanied a destructive giant of a man. They were never able to identify any ghost or relate them to any incidents, massacres or wars that raged around here. Legends tell of many stories of heroes and rogues, of love and hate, of intrigue and betrayal but although researchers examined all these stories they could not connect any person or incident with the grotesque terrors of Baleakin.'

'Have you a photograph of the house?' I asked.

'Aye, several,' said the Scot, 'and the book of the whole affair. Wait a moment and I'll dig out some photos.' He disappeared.

I felt suddenly to be alone and yet not alone. Unnerved I felt rushes of cold air and heard the skirting boards creaking as if something passed by. A noise like the tearing of shrouds seemed to be behind me. The distant rumblings and searchings of Alasdair echoed and re-echoed like movements in a vaulted tomb. Outside, the song of the birds became the wailing of souls in purgatory. The atmosphere was unwholesome and unworldly and my nerves almost reached breaking point when the very substantial Alasdair appeared.

'There's the hoose,' he said as he pointed to a photograph; 'and here's another. See that end bit? That's where we are sitting now. It was previously the servants' quarters and when the housebreakers had finished their work of demolition they left it standing.'

'When was it bulldozed?' I asked.

'Not so long ago. Certainly since the war. I should think in the sixties,' he replied.

It had been a most imposing house. I imagined it was fifteenth century at least and was built in the traditional highland way with corner turrets and buttresses and had been three storeys high with basement rooms.

'Let's gan oot and look around the rubble,' suggested Alasdair.

Together in single file we squeezed through the narrow alleys between the piles of books. Outside the sunshine was reassuring. There seemed to be no hint of ghosties, ghouls, warlocks and the like. Perhaps after demolition they had all found refuge in the Birks o' Aberfeldy. The Scot led me from the daylight to a lower room which had been a basement. Here there was a distinct evil atmosphere. It seemed to greet us with an embracing coldness. The dank stench of a vault permeated the darkened enclosure. I could feel the close proximity of the supernatural. I felt that something was clinging to my neck. It was a real feeling, not one of imagination. There was something there. Of that I am sure.

I hurried to get out and up again to where daylight showed everything in clear perspective.

'Alasdair, I felt uneasy down there. I imagined that something was clinging to my neck rather like a chiffon scarf and not a pair of hands.'

'It was not your imagination, Jack. I often go down there to keep it clear of vermin and every time I go the clinging sensation is felt by me. It was there that the worst of the happenings occurred. It was like a cesspond from which the terrors emanated. Down there the suicide joined the motley throng of phantoms. See that big stone? The laird had that cemented in place to block the only entrance. The demolition team tore it away to investigate but left that room untouched.'

Back in Alasdair's living room I asked him, 'Have you ever seen anything?'

He looked steadily at me. 'Would you like another lemon drink?' he asked.

'I'd love one, but have you ever seen anything?' I insisted.

'I'd rather not say,' the cautious Scot replied, and I could not get him to say yea or nay. However, he went on.

'After the house was knocked down they offered this bit to anyone free of rent. A few couples took advantage of the offer but none of them stayed for very long. They all flitted within a month.'

'How long have you been here and are you going to stay?' I enquired.

'Over four years and I'll bide here until I'm carried oot,' he insisted. It was time for me to leave.

'I hope that I can find my way out of here. I'd hate to be stranded. I'd rather be lost in the hills. I had difficulty in finding the place.'

'Aye; I'm no surprised,' he answered, 'Did you see anyone to ask for directions?'

I told him about the man up the hill who had been so kind.

'He's Geordie, "The Rabbit". I hope ye didna' mind his

swearing,' said Alasdair.

'Swearing? He didn't swear. He was most polite and helpful.'

'Disna' soond like Geordie. In fact he is a wealthy man but prefers to live up there. We call him "The Rabbit" because that is his main food. He catches them himself. It's done him no harm; he's eighty-eight,' said Alasdair who must have passed his own four-score years.

'Cheerio, and many thanks. I'm pleased to visit you but not to linger too long.'

'Come again, though,' he laughed, 'and bring your wife next time.'

I did! We found two chairs and we ate fresh fruit, ryebread and oatcakes, cheeses and honey and drank more lemon juice. We did not speak of ghosts. Perhaps they knew we were there and returned to the Birks o' Aberfeldy.

Trilogy Satanic

Black Ice

The westering sun cast long shadows between the gravestones and bathed the eastern wall of the church in darkness. A thrush trilled out its evening hymn of thanksgiving from the tall chestnut tree. Gnats patterned the air in dancing groups while the swallows gratefully feasted upon them.

'I'm sorry, Rector, to have called you out on a Saturday evening but come and see,' said Mrs Smith the church caretaker.

She was a diligent and reliable woman. Her duties at the church were not merely a job but rather her joy. She was entirely dedicated. It was *her* church and she loved it. Now she was deeply hurt and offended.

She hurried on before me to the western wall which was

topped by a slender steeple.

'Look,' as she almost cried.

A small pre-Reformation window had been shattered and entry to the church effected through it.

Saddened at the sight and feeling a surge of anger I was now led to the main door. Hanging from its handle was the mutilated and bloodless corpse of my own white cockerel which had gone missing overnight and which I had thought to be a victim of the foxes.

'We'll not go in until the police arrive,' I said to Mrs Smith, 'You haven't been in, have you?'

'No, Rector, I have only peeped in through the broken window and believe me there's a mess inside.'

'Let's walk around the outside. We may see something,' I suggested.

Two weeks earlier I had conducted old Duncan's funeral. His grave now looked disturbed. The fading wreaths had been slung to one side and the soil seemed to have been levelled. I descended into the boiler house to discover further upheaval there and a pile of ashes even though the place had been cleaned up during the week.

The police followed me into the church. Soil from Duncan's desecrated grave had been scattered down the aisle. An untidy heap of prayer books lay near the font. The pages containing the *Nunc Dimittis* had been torn from every book and as we never found them they must have been consigned to the boiler flames. Broken slivers of stained glass lay where they had fallen beneath the medieval window. The altar linen was bloodstained probably by the blood of my cockerel. The brass cross which I had donated and which had travelled the world with me in my navy days stood in the centre of the altar distorted and twisted out of recognition. Black candlegrease smudged the reredos. Hassocks had been tumbled about. In the vestry there was chaos, and attempts had obviously been made to force open the safe.

'Been after a chalice,' said the police inspector, 'There is no doubt that there has been a black mass!'

Two policemen helped Mrs Smith to clean up while the inspector and I examined the outside of the church. Apart from the disturbed grave and the ashes in the boiler house we found no further clues, but the next morning Flossie, our beloved headmistress provided one.

'I had a class of young children in the churchyard on Friday. We were combining a little local history with a nature talk. It was a lovely sunny day,' she began. Flossie is one of the nicest persons one could ever hope to meet and an asset to both the village and the church.

'I saw a man leave his car by the gate and come up to the church. He tried the church door but found that it was locked.

'If you'd like to see in the church, sir, I'll send one of my scholars to Mrs Smith for the key. It won't take a minute,' I offered.

'Instead of receiving a courteous reply he told me to go to hell,' related Flossie. Wisely she sent a scholar to obtain the registration number of the car. The police traced the number, and interviewed the owner.

He admitted that he had been at Great Stainton but had been tired after a long journey. He claimed that he was travelling from Glasgow to Manchester, felt drowsy, saw this quiet country church and decided to rest in it.

He was upset when he saw children 'galivanting about'.

Glasgow to Manchester? Great Stainton is near the North East coast and to the River Tees. The memory of this came flooding back to me nearly thirty years later, when two weeks ago I heard the following story.

Ice Cold

'You're early, Jack; not that you're ever late,' commented the superintendent of the crematorium.

'I could have been sooner but I had to fill the car up with petrol. The salesman at the garage was telling me that he'd served in the navy on hospital ships,' I replied.

'I think he's still injecting dope into my tank,' muttered

Gavin.

'Talking of hospital ships, Gavin, how's your pregnant fish?' I enquired.

Before a previous funeral Audrey, Gavin's wife, had invited me into their house which lay just inside the main gates of the cemetery.

'Like a cup of coffee, Jack?' she had asked, 'I've got some Greek brandy I could put in it; in fact; it's from Corfu.'

While it was being prepared I had walked to the recess in the fireside wall to look at the fish tank. In the corner of the tank was an aquatic maternity clinic cleverly designed to prevent newly born fish from becoming immediate bait for other predatory occupants of that small watery world. As I watched the brilliant displays from the tropical fish I enquired about the clinic.

'That fish is pregnant. She should produce within forty-eight hours. That's why we have trapped her in that unit. See the V shape? It's to keep her and others from devouring the young as they are born,' instructed Gavin.

So now, two weeks later, before another funeral, I enquired about the fish.

'Oh,' said Gavin, 'It wasn't pregnant. It had a phantom pregnancy.'

A fish with a phantom pregnancy boggled my imagination.

'Have you ever seen a pregnant cucumber?' enquired Ken, Gavin's assistant.

Young Paul answered, 'I have,' as Gavin hurled a blank memorial plaque at him.

'Hold hard,' I said, 'I have.' This I could truthfully assert. This discourse on the beginnings of life was taking place in the cemetery office, when Gavin said, 'Jack, you've reminded me; my car needs filling up. I'll pop across to the garage. By the way, Jack, after this funeral I want to tell you something very private. So knock on the house door when you're ready.'

He went to a tall, steel cabinet, unlocked it to reveal shelves of unfilled urns and removed the lid from one of them to retrieve his wallet.

'Can't be too careful around here,' he remarked. So the superintendent of Crowtrees Crematorium went for petrol and I donned my robes to go the the chapel.

Old Bella, whose funeral service I was now to conduct, had passed away at the advanced age of 96 years. Born in 1892 she had lived through perhaps the most momentous century of history. She had lived in six reigns. Horse drawn drays had not yet yielded to juggernauts or the magic lantern to the cinema and television. Dr Crippen had not yet been arrested on the high seas, through the wonder of radio. Bustles accentuated the female form, not the skin-tight jeans of today. Lacy bodices caught the eye rather than slogan-emblazoned T shirts. A gracious age indeed and yet Bella had never married and her daughter had also remained a spinster, yet her grandchildren had legalized things to provide surnames for the great grandchildren.

As Bella's coffin was being lifted from the hearse by the underbearers to be carried into the chapel Jane-Ann, her daughter, now over seventy years of age, seemed to be unusually distressed. I went across to her and put my arm around her shoulders in consolation.

'Vicar,' she said between heavy sobs, 'I'm terribly worried.'

'Why?' I enquired.

'Mother is deaf and they've taken away her hearing aid,' she cried looking towards the coffin.

I thought for a quick moment and then said; 'Don't worry, Jane-Ann, I'll speak up.'

I did. It made her happy.

I knocked at the door of Gavin's house. 'Come in, Jack,' invited Audrey, 'like a cup of coffee?'

'Splendid; I could do with one. I've just shouted that service.'

'Sorry there's no Corfu brandy left. Had the gas men here laying a new pipe. They liked it without the coffee,' said Audrey.

I sat as the fish in the tank made grotesque faces at me.

Gavin came in. It was half past four and winter time, when the nights are long and the days are short. The fire cast a warming glow and the coffee an inner glow.

'Now, Jack,' said Gavin, as we settled down to listen to his tale. 'This actually happened and we have told no one. It happened only the other evening.'

He seemed to glance nervously towards the shadows which grew about the darkened corners of the room. Our shadows cast by the firelight were long and crooked as they lay across the floor and climbed the walls. Audrey sat beside him on the settee holding his hand and scarcely lifting her eyes. The room went quiet and solemn and even the fish ceased to gulp.

'I was about to close the office up the other evening. The furnace man had already gone. I put the phone through to the house, locked the cupboards and was ready to come over to my home. Just then there was a timid knock on the office door. I felt irritated. The office hours were clearly displayed on the outer door. Why couldn't people see that it was now beyond business hours.'

' "Come in," I called. In came a vicar. You know him Jack. He told me his name and parish and I knew him well. He was well respected and nearing retirement age.

'He seemed agitated.

' "Sit down, Vicar. Have a cigarette". He sat but was plainly very nervous.

' "Will you do me a favour?" the vicar asked me.

' "If I can I will," I promised.

' "I have left a bin-liner bag on the grass outside. Will you cremate it for me?"

' "Well," I said cautiously, "it all depends. The crematorium is not an incinerator. I'll have to look inside to see its contents."

' "Don't look inside," the vicar said with deliberate emphasis. "There's evil in that bag. Just burn it as soon as you can; tonight if possible. I want this lot destroyed from the face of the earth."

'I was taken aback by his vehemence. His face betrayed

his fear; a real fear of something beyond his control.

' "The police have co-operated with me in investigating a black magic sect," he began in explanation. His agitation made his words come quickly and breathlessly.

' "Their temple was raided. A number have been arrested, both male and female. Articles used in their satanic rituals are in that bag. Believe me, it's evil. Don't tamper or delay. Get rid of it. I know what I'm saying. I've not only studied the subject I've witnessed it. Be careful; don't unleash the fury of Satan."

'I pondered. this seemed to be so unreal. If it had been you, Jack, I would have thought it to be some lark, but not with this vicar. He was serious and dead serious. I could hear the office clock ticking away the moments.

' "I'll tell you what to do," said the vicar, "ring the police. Verify my story and the urgency. In fact I'd rather you did ring them. It'll keep things right. They advised me to get the things cremated."

'I hesitated. I dialled the police. They confirmed the vicar's story and offered to come down to witness the burning. I decided to comply but without police presence.

' "Don't open the bag and do not take it into your house," advised the vicar.

' "It'll have to wait until the morning," I said, "as all the cremators are closed down."

' "Alright," said the cleric, "but don't take that bag into your house and do not look inside."

'After he had left I went out and in the fading light saw the bag lying on the grass by the flower bed. It looked harmless enough so I lifted it and deposited it in the scullery which is below our bathroom.'

The fire had burnt low and a distant street lamp scarcely invaded the room with light. Audrey was nestled so closely to Gavin that I could scarcely see her. The world outside was muffled and spectral since the window looked towards the graves.

Gavin continued. 'After tea Audrey decided to have a bath. She lay relaxed in the steaming water to enjoy her

70

ablutions. Condensation misted the tiles and humidity clouded the mirror. Suddenly thick ice coated the window and ice formed on the surface of the bath water. The temperature fell below zero at a rush. Audrey went blue with cold and was seized as if with a cramp. She couldn't move, paralysed by fear and cold. She screamed. I heard her shouts as I sat here. I tore up the staircase two stairs at a time and stormed into the bathroom. It seemed as if I had entered the arctic. The bathroom hung in icicles. It's true, Jack, I not only saw it, I felt it.'

He paused. Audrey shivered.

'I dashed downstairs into the scullery while Audrey was shouting "Come back; come back," and I picked up the black bag and hurled it into the cemetery. When I reached the bathroom again all was normal. Steam still rose from the bathwater and the window was misted with condensation. Audrey wasn't there. I found her beneath the bedclothes!'

'What an amazing story and terrifying experience,' I remarked.

'Ah,' continued Gavin, 'the next morning I retrieved the

bag and took it to the cremator chamber. I was tempted to look inside the bag. Should I? Shouldn't I? I did! I was scared. Only for a fleeting moment did I peer in and all I saw lying on top of unrecognisable items were the talons of an eagle's severed foot. One more peculiar feature about this; after cremation there were no remains, not even an ash. All had been consumed without leaving any trace.'

On my way home that night I saw a number of black plastic bin-liners filled with rubbish outside the old people's home waiting for collection by the bin men. I shuddered.

White Hot

McClusky was his name; not his real name which was Polish and unpronounceable. The matron at the old people's home was noting his particulars on an admission form.

'Can you spell that name for me?' she asked.

It seemed as if every letter of the alphabet had been mixed inextricably and then suffixed with 'ski'.

With great initiative she said, 'We'll call you Mr McClusky; it's near enough.

He grunted, no doubt in Polish.

'Now, what's your religion?' she asked.

'Satanist,' was his startling answer.

'Satanist? We can't put that down. I'll put C. of E.; that will cover it.'

So Mac, the Pole who was baptized into the Church of Rome and had defected to the arch enemy was now recorded as my responsibility.

'Hello,' I said, introducing myself, 'I'll come straight to the point. Why describe yourself as a Satanist?'

'Because I am,' he bluntly asserted.

'It's easy to say so, but surely you don't mean it,' I insisted.

A devilish glint came into his eye. He leaned close to me. I could feel the fire of his breath.

'I've sold my soul to the devil!' he said as he crossed

himself in reverse.

I lowered my gaze, fearful of detecting brimstone. I could see his feet. They were not cloven but encased in sloppy carpet slippers.

So he insisted to everyone, doctor, matron, care-attendants and chaplain. The R.C. priest came to see him and returned to his presbytery to implore the protection of St. Michael and his angels.

McClusky was dying. Two care-attendants and the night porter were closetted in the small staff room. It was near to midnight. Joe, the porter, arrested the course of his teacup towards his mouth.

'Did you hear that?'

'No,' said Mavis, 'What?'

'Just listen,' said Joe quietly.

There was silence. All was still and they listened. Then, distinct but subdued, they heard the bleating of a goat.

Jacqui shivered. 'Someone's just walked over my grave.'

'More like McClusky's grave. The noise is coming from his room,' Mavis whispered.

'Let's go and see,' said Jacqui, 'Joe, you go first.'

There was no rush. Joe polluted his coffee with inhaled cigarette smoke. He was delaying action by pretending to concentrate his hearing. Then he led the crawl to Mac's room. He was dead!

Eventually duly cleansed with hands piously crossed over his chest as if in supplication, McClusky was loaded on a trolley for transportation to the mortuary.

'Jack, I don't expect you to believe this but it's true. Mavis here will verify it.' We were again in the staff room but they were now on day-shift.

'Last week,' began Joe, 'when McClusky died, I took his body to the mortuary. When I got there I opened the refrigerated drawer. Suddenly the drawer was white-hot! The heat made me shield my eyes. I felt as if I was being scorched. There were no flames; just this fierce heat. In panic I ran dragging the trolley behind me with Mac still on it.'

He paused, evidently scarcely believing his own story.

'I told Mavis. We entered the episode in the log book. I was pleased when our shift finished. The day staff rang the undertaker who took poor old Mac to a chapel of rest. What happened, if anything, at the chapel I don't know. Our electrician examined the wiring at the mortuary and found it to be in order.'

'Who officiated at the funeral?' I asked.

'Don't know. I wanted nothing to do with it. No one went from here,' said Mavis.

I rang the funeral director. He didn't know. 'It was taken out of my hands.'

Finally, as none of the staff would go to the mortuary again whether by day or night, its use has been discontinued.

Ice cold in the crematorium; white-hot in the mortuary; are the seasons changing?

No Footprints

'I'm hame, Mary,' called George Pattison as he settled into an upright wooden chair before the fire. 'What about a brew-up? It's varry cold oot there.'

Mary called back from the distant kitchen. 'Won't be a minute, just doing the lamps. Put the kettle on the fire.'

Mary had cleaned the glass funnels during the morning but now as the fitful light of Old Year's Day allowed the shadows to deepen beyond the range of the fireglow, she was trimming the wicks and replenishing the oil. When she came into the parlour with a lamp, the kettle was already singing. Carefully she placed the lamp on the wide ledge of the dresser. She made a paper spill and obtained a flame from the fire which she applied to the lampwick. She let it slumber in a narrow, uncertain flicker before turning up the wick so giving a warming glow chasing away the shadows.

No Footprints

It was New Year's Eve! George shifted his gaze from the steaming mug of tea cupped in his hands to the smouldering logs of the fire. Mary preferred a cup and sat on the other side of the hearth. She still wore her long, white pinafore.

'George, looking back over the year, what was your saddest day?' she asked.

Still contemplating the curling smoke and the occasional flicker of flame George was silent as he recollected. 'May day, without a doubt.'

'May day' on the Borders was not May 1st with all its romancing and dancing and Maypoles. It was May 12th; the traditional day of the 'flittings'. Many a sad farewell was spoken that day as farm workers loaded carts with all their worldly goods and with their families departed to new homes and work under new masters. This crisis in the lives of the agricultural families was known as 'The May'.

'I hate to see the lines of carts upon our roads that day. We've been fortunate in that our workers have been content to stay with us, but it was a shock, Mary, when John Oxley decided to flit after all these years.'

'You were like brothers,' remarked Mary. 'I helped to bring three of their bairns into the world. Fiona was a strong woman and would be back in the fields three days after childbirth. I made the cheese and you gave the whisky when those bairns were born.'

'Aye, it was sad to see them going. John had the cart and Fiona led the cow. I offered to help but they were so independent. I'd have them back if they would come.'

'I wonder where she got that hat with the long, white feather stuck in it,' queried Mary with womanly interest, 'but what was your happiest day?'

'I always enjoy the kirn-dance. It was funny this year. Ian Taylor was so drunk; he talked to the kirn-dolly for an hour before asking it to go into the byres with him. Then the sexton, Bob Charlton grew bold and asked Moira to marry him.'

'Oh I didn't know that,' protested Mary, 'she must have

said no.'

'Wouldn't you too if a suitor proposed by asking how you would like to see your name on his tombstone,' laughed George.

He stirred the fire into a warming glow, which lighted up the aged face of the grandfather clock. The clock was so old that it endured rheumatism in the weight-chains and so often ran slow. It said three-thirty although it was now after four o'clock.

'Mind you, Mary, that Jewish pedlar always made me laugh. I said to him, "What have you got this time? Anything for the lads, Reuben?" He had pictures of Pope Pius X in full pontificals and of Rabbie Burns in Masonic regalia. He did a roaring trade with tinselled madonnas and portraits of our Royal Family. He even had a potion to increase the virility of the farmhands. It was like selling snowballs to the eskimos.'

'And have you made any resolutions for 1903?'

'Aye,' said George, 'I've decided . . . oh, there's the bairns.'

The sound of children's voices hardly penetrated the solid, oak front door. George opened it. The frost was biting at the children's noses which peeped out of woollen helmets which also muffled the singing.

'Not a penny until you sing the Hogmanay,' said George. Their little voices took up the ancient songwords with gusto.

> 'Get up, guid wife and shake your feathers,
> and dinna think that we are beggars;
> we're little children come to play.
> Please give us our Hogmanay.
> May God bless all friends dear;
> A merry Christmas and happy New Year.'

So New Year's Eve 1902 became wrapped in darkness and mystery. As the grandfather clock wheezed half-past-eight it was half-past-nine. George came downstairs dressed in his Sunday best.

'I don't think that we'll get far afield tonight. The snow's too bad and we'll probably get only as far as the Bull at Etal. I know that a few of the men want to go to the Besom at Coldstream and have a cart all limbered up ready, but I'll not go with them.'

'Don't forget, you are our firstfoot tonight,' reminded Mary.

'I'm pleased ye mentioned that. Whatever you do divvent open the door te anyone at aal; and aa mean nebody; absolutely nebody. Only open up if you hear my voice. We divvent want any women fair-haired men or anyone flatfooted, to get in first. Remember, if anyone comes ask if I'm there too,' warned George.

'No one will cross this thresh until you come in. I'll leave some coal and sticks outside on a shovel. Keep sixpence in your pocket.'

In the lamplight Mary knitted for a while. She preferred the rocking chair and hummed as she gently swayed.

'The best bed, the feather bed
    the best bed of a'
The best bed i' wor hoose
    is clean pea-straw.'

She didn't want the clock to be behind for the New Year so she went to it and moved the hands on one hour. She guessed that it would be about right by midnight. Then she brought in another lamp for the middle of the table first having spread a fine linen cloth. On this she placed glasses, bottles of whisky, brandy, a blackcurrant wine, two bottles of home-made ginger wine, a fruit cake and plates. She took a sprig of holly from above the dresser and placed it by the cake. All looked warm and hospitable.

The old clock groaned the midnight hour. Mary checked it and according to George's gold hunter the old clock was on time. It was 1903!

As Mary turned away from the clock she heard a noise. Glancing at the front door, which was securely bolted at the top, bottom and midway, she was terrified to see the door handle turning slowly but surely. The door remained shut. The handle turned again and whoever was turning it shook the door in an endeavour to open it.

'Is that you, George?' called out a startled Mary. There was no answer but the doorknob gyrated furiously. Then there was a heavy pounding on the door and the knob fell, inwards as it was wrenched from the outside.

Mary was used to being alone at night in the house especially at lambing time when very often the lambing storm lashed the house and moaned down the chimney. Now she was terrified.

'Go away. Go away whoever you are. GO!' she yelled. There was silence. The grandfather clock had stopped altogether. The atmosphere inside felt bitterly cold despite the blazing fire. Mary hurriedly placed a stout chair against the front door then ran to the back door to make sure that it was secured. As she got there so did the unseen, unknown, unwelcome visitor. The sneck rattled and something or someone pushed against the door. It did not yield.

'Oh God, oh God, what is happening?' she cried. As the attempts to gain access ceased, Mary sank into her chair and shook. Greatly relieved she heard familiar voices outside.

'Is that you, George?' she anxiously enquired.

'Yes, Mary, with the lads from the Beaumont, the Tweed and the Till.' This was the arranged password; a quotation from a local ditty sung at 'booling' time.

Mary unbolted the door with trembling and fumbling fingers.

'Come on, lass; let's in,' came a chorus from frozen men. She fell sobbing into George's arms.

He kissed her and wished her a happy new year, then bent down and collected the coal and sticks. He placed them on the fire.

'Mary, you've not poured the drinks. Come on, lass, get cracking,' remonstrated the farmer.

'I canna; I canna. I'm trembling ower much. What a fright I've had.'

The drinks were poured, the toasts were drunk and Mary, somewhat reassured by the presence of the men, told her story.

George's brother, Gordon Pattison, who married Moira, Will Neil, Barry Carham and Patrick the soldier listened.

Then Gordon said, 'We had a shock too. If I hadna seen it wi' my own eye I would nivor have believed it.'

'What was it? asked Mary.

'There must be five inches o' snaw oot there yet a weird figure in a black cloak passed us as we came here. It came from the direction of Bob Charlton's cottage by the kirkyard. Will Neil said to me in a low whisper, "Look, Gordon, no footprints!" ' Will took up the story.

'We all looked and sure enough that figure left no footprints in the snow, whereas the snow came ower the tops o' wor boots. I called oot, "Guidneet, mate," but got no reply. It certainly was uncanny.'

'I reckon that's who tried to get into here,' suggested Mary.

The temperature was below zero at daybreak. Sheila was Bob Charlton's housekeeper. She came up to Mary's house before ten o' clock.

'Mary, I'd such a shock last night. I had to come round to tell you. Bob was at the church to toll the old year out and ring the new year in, when I heard the door open. An icy blast tore through the house. Cups and ornaments rattled. The clock stopped. It always does when there's going to be a death! I hurried to close the door and there, like a ghoulish scarecrow stood a figure covered from head to foot in black. I screamed. The thing, it didn't seem human, turned and walked away. Mary, you'll not believe me. It walked through the snow leaving no footprints. It's true, Mary; no footprints. The thing was from another world. It was evil. I've let bad luck into the house.'

'Dinna fash yersel,' Sheila. Nowt will happen. Anyway, you're scared of spiders, aren't you?'

'This is different. I'm convinced that this thing was the devil. It's bound to bring bad luck.'

Late in the afternoon Bob Charlton took a short cut across the rail track which went to Cornhill. He was anxious to reach home before dark. Head bent against the driving snow he did not see or hear the train approaching.

He was buried in his own churchyard on January 4th.

Foreign Phantom

It was January 2nd. Christmas bunting still straddled Kingsway in Valletta and Santa Claus still beamed from posters designed to impoverish the susceptible. The only snow Malta had was whitewash or plastic·sprayed on the window panes. All this looked rather jaded and woe-begone as a sudden, heavy rain shower blasted in from the sea. It was a cold rain and had caught me unprepared and without a raincoat.

God, who I think must be a presbyterian missioner, sent the first few drops of rain to fall upon me in South Street right outside the Church of Scotland. As it's any port in a storm I hurried into the church; I hope with John Knox's approval. I averted my eyes away from the free-will offering box which, in any case, was the undisturbed home of a hermit spider, and selected a pew near to the door. I could hear the rain pounding on the windows as it descended with tropical force. I bowed my head in silent prayer remembering my loved ones at home This reminded me that I had in my pocket a letter I had received just that morning. I took it from my inside pocket to re-read it. In it my wife told me that John Yorke had invited me to visit him if our ship ever went into the Persian Gulf.

I had known John in years gone by. I remembered the early buses. They carried twelve to fourteen passengers with difficulty and were constructed so high upon their chassis that a rope ladder would have greatly facilitated boarding. Then in opposition, the Blue Buses began to operate on the same routes. John was appointed inspector of these magnificent new omnibuses. In the days when one could gain admission to the cinema matinee by presenting three empty jam-jars at the box office, fare dodging on the old buses was the acclaimed skill of the wide-boys. John Yorke's peaked cap scared them and led them to walk or to embrace penury.

Evidently certain burnoused Arabs were fiddling their ackers on the camel caravans of Saudi Arabia. John, who did not know the language or the coinage was appointed transport manager of a well-known international oil company, in the Persian Gulf. So he packed his bags, timetables and excess fare tickets, and donned his peaked cap to depart for the rich pickings of the oil fields.

'That peaked cap is no good for over there,' I said, 'It has no ventilation.'

'It's all I've got,' complained John.

Jack in the Spirit

'Ah,' I said, scenting a financial boost to my depleted reserves, 'I have the very thing for you. I've a pith helmet with a fan in the roof. I'll get it to see if it will fit you.' John left these shores with my pith helmet and a quantity of 'pusser's' surplus tropical rig; double spined shirts, and Bombay shorts which in those days of modesty covered the knee!

My last home leave had coincided with his first break from the heat of the Gulf.

'How's life out there, John?' I asked.

'Great; and the money's fantastic. I get as much in one month as I did in six months here. I love the work and the people, but I have a story for you,' replied John.

'Of wine, dusky maidens and song, no doubt,' I suggested.

'No such luck. Out there it's non-alcoholic. Dusky maidens actually risk their very lives if they follow the world's oldest profession. No. It's a real-life ghost story,' he said.

We sat in the garden as he related this story to me.

'The company built a super, modern bungalow for Joan and me. Until it was ready we lived in an hotel for about six months.'

He gave me a fistful of photographs of the new bungalow. It was superb. Its rooms were spacious. A veranda graced the south and west walls. It had every modern convenience.

'The company furnished it and we moved in. It was a housewife's dream,' he said. 'During the first night of our occupation, John, our son, who is now four years of age, came into our bedroom.

' "Daddy, I'm frozen. Can I come into your bed?" he asked. I thought that perhaps he felt a little strange and needed the assurance of our presence. The same thing happened the following night and continued for two weeks.

' "You'll have to settle down and stay in your own bed tonight, John", I told him.

' "I'll try," he agreed, "but take that Arab away from my room."

82

' "There's no Arab in your room; you're dreaming it.'

' "No, Daddy; he brings the cold."

' "I'll tell you what," I suggested to him, "I'll sleep in your room tonight. You can sleep with mammy."

'This was arranged. I was tired. The night was warm and humid but I felt that I would sleep like a log. Within minutes I was fast asleep in John's bed. Then I awoke. It was the intense cold that had awakened me. I was actually shivering and shook a lot more when I saw an Arab standing at the foot of the bed dressed in a white winding sheet! I sat up, my teeth chattering with both cold and fear. No words would come to my lips. I admit that it was terrifying. The ghost didn't vanish; I did,' concluded John.

'What happened than?' I asked.

'The company discovered that the bungalow had been erected on an old burial site for Arabs. We returned to the hotel to live and the bungalow was dismantled and rebuilt on a different site,' said John.

I pondered on this as I sat in the pew when I was startled.

'You did give me a fright, sir. I thought you were the doctor,' said a scared lady who had tip-toed up to me.

'I'm the church cleaner,' she declared and went on to give me a brief summary of her life.

'I was born and bred in Sicily. After the war I married a soldier of the Black Watch. We went to live in Aberdeen. I loved the people and the place but the cold was not pleasant. Still, I was happy with my husband. He was a good man and had settled in civilian life as a security officer.'

Due no doubt to a draughty kilt and a distillery strike her husband had died of pneumonia and dehydration. She had adopted her husband's presbyterian persuasion and the Church, upon her widowhood, offered her a house in Malta if she took on the task of church cleaner.

'Who is the doctor you thought that I might be?' I asked her.

'Was; not is,' she corrected me.

'He was a doctor here in Malta. He worked at St. Luke's hospital in Sleima. He was the session clerk at this church and rarely missed a service or meeting,' she told me.

'A veritable pillar of strength,' I remarked.

'Indeed and it was a sad blow to us when he died suddenly after a massive coronary,' she sighed.

'Well, if he is dead, what made you think that I was the doctor?' I asked.

'You see, sir, he comes back every day and sits in this very pew! He sits quietly for about half an hour and then just isn't here.'

'When does he come?' I enquired.

'About now. That's why I thought that you were him.'

That's when I thought it was time for me to go!

The Verger's Visitors

The slight breeze gently wafted the bride's veil across her mother's features at the precise moment the cameras went 'click' much to the bridegroom's delight and the irritation of the mother. The result would probably be that the woman looked like an ethereal manifestation, clad in a green which was indistinguishable from the dense crop of weeds behind her, and a head that belonged to beyond the veil. The photographer quickly folded his tripod and in his hurry almost fell over the pony club contingent. An elderly couple had lingered to watch these proceedings and I was there, not as the incumbent, but in the hope that I might sting my friend the verger for a cup of coffee.

'It brings memories flooding back, Sal' said old Ned who had taken those vital steps up the aisle more than fifty years previously.

'Aye, but don't remind me,' then addressing me, Sal went on, 'The car broke down so I was twenty minutes late arriving at the church. The vicar wasn't too pleased as he was a football fanatic; the best man had placed the wedding ring on his little finger and couldn't remove it when it was required as his finger had swollen, the vicar called me Jane instead of Sarah and a shower hit us as we left the church.'

'I laughed when your uncle in his speech referred to you as Calamity Jane and said that he feared for my future safety in the house. Happy day, but then the past fifty years have been happy too,' admitted Ned.

'The vicar called me Jane until his dying day and the calamity tag stuck,' remarked Sarah, alias Sal alias Calamity.

'We're just going into the church to see the flowers,' Sal concluded.

'I'll walk up with you,' I said.

We walked on rose-leaf, heart and cupid confetti despite a notice which read, 'Dogs and confetti not allowed in this churchyard.' There seemed to be however no prohibition on horses.

Bob, the verger, almost collided with us as we entered the church porch. He was hurriedly leaving it carrying a dustpan filled with horse droppings!

'Where're you going with that, Bob?' I asked. 'It's good for rhubarb.'

'No fear. Old Tom Smith's grave needs a top dressing,' answered Bob.

'Where did it come from?' I enquired.

'From a horse, of course,' snapped Bob.

'I know that; but was it in church?'

'Yes.'

'You had a cuddy in the church?' asked Ned.

Bob explained to us as the aroma of fresh manure assailed our nostrils and the stench of the stable began to fill the porch.

'The bride came to church riding side saddle on her favourite horse. While they were signing the register in the vestry some misguided groom, I mean horse-groom not bridegroom, brought the horse into church to greet them. The horse made a free-will offering! It wasn't house trained or church trained. This is what it left behind and the bride's mother exulted, "Praise the Lord, this is a symbol of good luck". It may be for them but not for me. I'll have to scrub that carpet and get an air freshener.'

'Well, go and put it on Tom Smith's grave before it loses its potency. He'll appreciate it. He never did agree with chemicals or artificial manures. Then come across to your cottage and we'll have a chat,' I suggested.

'Right ho. Give me a quarter of an hour and I'll be ready. Go into the church and see the flowers but be careful where you tread,' warned Bob.

Bob had made his cottage really comfortable and pleasant. As we chatted there was a resounding thump on his front door. Bob never moved but yelled, 'Come in, the door's open,' then to me in a quiet voice, 'this will be Derek, my brother.'

Derek, his wife and young daughter Rachel came in.

'We thought that we would call on you before we went off on our holiday to Minorca,' Derek explained and then while Eileen, Derek's wife, began making the coffee we settled down to a cheerful conversation.

Eileen said over her coffee cup, 'Vicar, do you know anything about ghosts? I mean, do you believe in them?'

'Yes,' I admitted, 'do you know of one?'

'We were terribly troubled in our last house, but the story is so involved that it will have to wait until we come back from our holiday,' said Eileen.

They came back from the Mediterranean bronzed and brought me a cigar ashtray, and Bob several little gifts including a dustpan and soft handbrush!

'Now, what about that ghost?' I requested.

'Ghosts, not one, I've written it all down for you. This account both Derek and I swear is absolutely true. I'll leave it with you.'

Here is Eileen's story.

'In March 1972 I was given the chance of a small, two-bedroomed, upstairs flat. We were to be married the following July so naturally I was pleased with the offer

86

offer and we wasted no time in going around to view it.
We suspected a certain amount of dampness as there was
a foisty smell but we learned that it had been empty for
ten years. Why a perfectly sound flat had remained
empty for so long was not a question that bothered us as
we were so delighted to have somewhere to set up home.
Some time previously someone had begun to strip the
walls of the wallpaper but had only completed one room
and had left the others untouched. I did wonder about
this but we went ahead in renting the premises with the
future hope of buying it. Eagerly we set about decorating
it to our taste.

I experienced a strange sensation which I could not
explain either to myself or to anyone else. Every room
was unnaturally cold. I thought that perhaps it was my
imagination but despite increased heating the rooms
remained cold. We moved in after our honeymoon.
Everything seemed to be well and Derek and I were
extremely happy.

Then things began to happen! Derek was working late.
I arrived home at about 10.30 pm. I opened the door and
hurried up the stairs to switch on the electric light. I
entered the sitting room and closed the door behind me.
I filled the kettle and was placing the tea cups on the
occasional table when the room door crashed open with
such violence that it bounced back again as it hit the
edge of the settee. I was startled. Not even a strong wind
would have crashed that door open in such a manner as
the ballcatch was extremely stiff and one had to push
very hard with full body weight to open it. My impelling
curiosity overcame my fear and I went to the landing at
the top of the stairs to see if anyone was there.

To my abject horror I saw the outline of a figure
leaning with both hands on the door that opened on to
the back stairs.'

At this crucial point of Eileen's account my own back
door opened vigorously and a voice echoed through my

room. Startled, I hurried to the door and saw a figure leaning on the kitchen cabinet. It was Gavin kindly delivering eggs.

'I rang but got no answer,' Gavin explained, 'so I was about to leave these eggs on the cabinet.'

We had a lighthearted conversation mainly touching the subject of my entry into the garden competition.

'You'll win the booby prize,' foretold Gavin.

'What is it?' I asked in expectation.

'A load of manure,' he laughed. Then with his cargo of hen fruit he sped off to spread more high cholesterol to the immediate populace. I returned to the reading of Eileen's account. I re-read, 'To my horror I saw the outline of a figure!' Then I read on.

'My immediate thought was to get out of the house as quickly as my quaking legs would carry me. At this point the television set lost its picture for no apparent reason. I ran down the stairs and out of the house. Behind me there seemed to be something that was malevolent, overpoweringly evil and destructive. I could feel the presence almost smothering me until I reached the street. Frantically I thundered on the door of the downstairs flat. The young couple there calmed me and I told them of the terrible experience. Michael, the young husband offered to check the house and make sure that no one was lurking in its shadows. He had been gone scarcely ten minutes when he returned ashen white. He was extremely agitated and at first quite speechless.

"I will never go into that house again," he said.

"Why?" asked his anxious wife.

"I cannot tell you. I would never have believed it. It was horrible!"

"What was?" his wife insisted.

"I cannot tell you. I won't tell you; but we aren't staying here. To think that only a thin wall separates us from that." said Michael.

He never did tell us and he never again entered our flat.

"I saw a shadowy outline actually pass through our wall into your flat the other day. It would come out on your stairs. I was scared but persuaded myself that it had never happened," said Ellen, Michael's wife.

When Derek arrived home he did his best to reassure

me but his assurance was short-lived. Trinkets and ornaments began to move about. I went shopping one day and upon my return the state of our living room was chaotic. Heavy furniture had been moved, and ornaments rearranged but there was nothing damaged. Somehow I learned to live with it.

Derek began to notice that things were truly happening and that it was not merely my imagination or state of nerves. Among other things noticed by him

were the sweet smells which at times pervaded the flat.
Somehow I thought that perhaps my pregnancy was
exciting either opposition or distress to whatever spirit
still roamed about our home. So it was that when I
returned home with my baby, Rachel, I hoped that the
ghostly troubles would cease. Michael and Ellen
downstairs moved away from the neighbourhood and
Derek decided to purchase both flats and convert them
into one dwelling house. Secretly I believed that the
extensive alterations to the geography of the house would
spell the end of the haunting. When the builders had
completed their work we moved back into what was now
one, pleasant, spacious house. My hopes were soon
dashed!

The baby would not settle in her bedroom. I could
often hear a baby crying and would hurry up to Rachel's
room to find her fast asleep and the crying still
continuing. The temperature in that room was always
cold even though the central heating was checked for
efficiency.

Things began to worsen. The freezer switched itself off
and actually deplugged itself. I heard heavy breathing on
the stair landing yet no one other than myself was in the
house. My sister and her friends called around for tea
one day and as my sister went upstairs to the toilet the
light switch began to operate on and off. We all heard a
baby cry upstairs even though Rachel was with us in the
living room. Two or three of us went upstairs to
investigate feeling that there was safety in numbers but
before we reached the bedroom the crying stopped. After
this occasion our popularity took a dive. No one would
baby sit for us. Our friends stayed away and even our
relatives would not stay alone in the house.

Things were so bad that I consulted my doctor. He
recommended a visit to our vicar. The vicar listened to
our story most sympathetically. He prayed with us and
promised to call round the following evening.

In a moving service the vicar exorcised the house.

When he invoked the Name of the Trinity, Father, Son and Holy Spirit, there came a series of loud and violent thumps over our heads! I was terrified. These bangings lasted for over ten minutes during which we all prayed silently and my prayers were perhaps more fervent than they had ever been before. When the deafening noise ceased, the vicar suggested that when a person dies in evil circumstances they cannot progress to their true spiritual home. They become trapped and then trouble begins which we recognise as hauntings. If the house has been the scene of evil or distress a bad atmosphere is created. I eventually found out that a baby had died in the boxroom and also that an elderly man had been killed as he either fell or was pushed down the stairs.

I could no longer live in that house. The past associations of the fifteen years which we had endured in it became too much for me. A black cloud of mystery and misery seemed to hang about the place and for the last six years had become really oppressive.

We moved out and as we were actually moving I felt that something or someone was trying to prevent us from going. I am now extremely happy and carefree in our new home and I never go near to the old place!'

Longhirst

'See that little green gate in the wall? That's where the Longhirst ghost enters,' Bob Grey indicated with his left hand.

He was a passenger in my car as I travelled towards Ulgham and my daughter's home. He had requested a lift as far as Longhirst. He was a retired miner. He had enjoyed life to the full. He had worked hard, played hard and drank hard. He had graduated from a clay pipe to a briar and could still delve in his own garden even though he was eighty-five years old.

'I can remember,' he once told me, 'how a woman was set on at Longhirst pit. The manager was the nephew of the owner and he knew nowt about pits or men. The woman was desperately poor. She was tall and skinny, straight up and down. Dressed as a man she went to the colliery offices and asked for work. She looked like a man. Her name was Matilda and gave her name as Matt to the manager.'

'Did she get away with it?' I asked.

'Wey aye. Easy. We all knew that she was a woman and made life easy for her,' Bob added, 'but after five years a complication arose.'

'What was that?'

'After foreshift one day she went into the manager's office. "Yes, Matt", the young boss had asked "What do you want?"

' "My cards, please," replied Matilda.

' "What for? Got another job?"

' "No, sir. I'm pregnant."

'The manager was aghast. Was this to be the fulfilment of the prophecy that man born of man will live for ever?

' "Come again", he said. "What did you say?"

' "I'm going to have a baby, sir. I'm a woman."

'She had her bairn and eventually married the overman. He thought that he was the father of the baby but half a dozen other pitmen could have made the same claim.'

'Who or what is the Longhirst ghost?' I asked.

We had reached Bob's destination and sat in my car as Bob told his story.

'No one rightly knows who it is. It is reckoned that when one of the family from the Hall is to suffer calamity, bereavement or shock or that there would be a disaster at the pit the ghost will appear before the death or tragedy. It comes from the churchyard at midnight, walks across the road and enters into the Hall grounds through that gate.'

I walked back to the gate. It was small and stained with all the grime thrown up from the road so that its true colour was almost indiscernible. Obviously it had never been opened for a very long time. I climbed to the top of the wall and could see that no path led from that gate but if there had ever been a path it was now part of the jungle of weeds and brambles.

'Take more than a ghost to open this,' I remarked to Bob.

'Mebbe so,' he replied, 'but it was opened not long ago; by the ghost of course.'

'Has it been seen recently?'

The Hall was no longer the residence of the owners but served as a probation school.

'Not long ago. Old Tom Main was on backshift. He lived at Hebron and cycled to work. This particular night his front tyre was punctured just before he got to the Church bank. He had to push the bike and was hurrying up the hill when he saw it.'

'Saw what?' I asked.

'Wey man, the ghost!'

'Had he been drinking beforehand?' I asked.

'No way would Tom drink at any time. He is a Methodist local preacher and always as sober as a judge. He never got to work. Ne fear. He told me that he saw the Longhirst ghost. It was quite clear. It had features, not merely a skull, and dragged its graveclothes behind it. Tom said that it looked grey, but a peculiar kind of grey that was quite distinct in the darkness without it being luminous.

'It rose from the churchyard and seemed to float over the wall then it walked slowly looking steadfastly towards that gate. Tom gasped audibly but the spectre did not turn or falter but continued across the road. Its hand stretched out to open the gate, which swung open without a creak or hindrance. Then it looked at Tom. He saw it very clearly. The features were those of a man and were sad and forlorn. Before terror gripped him, Tom actually felt a deep sorrow for the spirit and watched until it disappeared in the grounds of the Hall.'

'What happened then?' I eagerly enquired.

'Tom disappeared too. Jumping on his bike he rode as if the furies were chasing him all the way back to Hebron. His front tyre was torn to shreds and the wheel buckled. Tom never used that road again,' said Bob.

'Was there any purpose in the ghost's walking that night? Did anything happen?'

'The very next day,' said Bob, 'the youngest son of the family was thrown from his horse and killed.'

'Thanks for the story, Bob. I'll check on it. Have others seen it?'

'As far as I know it's been appearing for a long time, long before my time and I'm well ower eighty.'

We had now reached Bob's cottage. 'Howay in,' he invited, 'the missus will make us some coffee. Anyway she likes company. We divvent see ower many people doon here.'

Bob's wife made their combined ages add up to one hundred and seventy years. She is an amazing lady. Her pinny was bright and girding it about her she soon produced coffee and scones.

'Bob; get that poem out of the dresser and let Mr Richardson read it,' she said. We were settled on an old horsehair sofa and Bob read the poem to me rather than risk the frail, brown paper backed booklet to my hands.

'First let me tell you that it was written by a farm hand from Bothal called William Gall. I never met him but I know that he used to cycle for miles around this countryside and compose his poems on location,' began Bob.

I do not know when his poems were published and I have strenuously endeavoured to ascertain if there is any copyright, without success. I understand that Mr Gall has been dead for many years. If he has any relatives I do not wish to infringe their rights.

The preface to his book of poems and stanzas refers to him as someone who observes nature in all her glory; from the rising of the sun to its going down; winding streams and mossy fells are depicted with a truthfulness and simplicity indicating that nature-love abounds and abides in the breast of the author of these surprisingly appreciative verses. Animate and inanimate are described with verve and swing and the perusal by any nature lover will well reward the reader with more than a glimpse of the everyday history of country life.

Bob adjusted his spectacles to a reading position from the end of his nose, sipped at his coffee and read the poem to me as it should be read, with a rich, pleasing Northumbrian burr.

The Longhirst Ghost

Lone intruder of the night,
Clad in flowing robes of white;
Noiseless passing through the porch
That stands near by the village church.

Flitting onward, there you go,
Weird ill-omen of future woe,
Heeding not the traveller's tread,
Restless spirit of the dead.

Jack in the Spirit

Departed soul; now can it be
Transactions wild that troubles thee:
Wert thou involved in wicked crime
which sends thee forth from time to time?

Can not thy guilty conscience find
Somewhere to rest thy troubled mind;
Or art thou caused by Higher Power
To flit alone at midnight hour?

Darkness throws a dismal gloom
O'er haunted vale and lonely tomb;
When fiercesome storms are raging past
Thy slender form rides on the blast.

No haven of rest the soul can win
that sank submerged in depths of sin;
To fall in guilt means grief and woe,
So spirits fled may flit below.

William Gall.

Fey

We had exchanged the wig-wams of our training centre
for the palatial extravaganza of Warblington House. We
toured its many rooms; the inevitable Blue Room and the
room that really won my admiration, the Singapore Room,
the decor and furnishings of which all came from the Far
East. During our stay there we were temporally deprived of
dehydrated egg and cardboard slivers of spam. Here was
the real McCoy!

After our first dinner there we sat in the library. We used
this room each evening because of its many advantages.

It had the most effective black-out shutters; it was adjacent to the air-raid shelter and its leather chairs were sumptuously embracing. I further favoured it because it had books. I sat reading *The Life of Nelson*, never dreaming in that wartime haven that in later years I would be a successor to Nelson's relative as vicar of a Northumberland parish.

There were six of us. Vic who was probably a relative of mine; Mac who I loved as a brother, Robbie tall and friendly, J. R. Rowley, the other J. R. and Bob Foreman who was the oldest of us all. Mac, the philosopher, perused the reference section and took down a volume. Opening it at random he spoke. 'Do you know that only nine and a half percent of flies die at the hands, or should I say legs and jaws, of spiders?'

I wondered how it was that we had managed to survive so long in this competitive world in total ignorance of this stupendous fact. Now, strengthened by such information we could confidently go forth in our struggle against the powers of darkness. I hoped that Hitler had not read that amazing passage. How do the other flies die? Mac didn't give us the answer. Provoking! Robbie, being tall, searched the top shelves for comics but found none so he consulted Wisden's Cricket Almanack.

As I read I felt that someone was gazing at me! I did not feel uncomfortable as I had when a psychiatric patient in a bed opposite to mine in a casualty hospital in Bristol sat upright in his bed for three days with a fixed, glaring stare fastened upon me. It never wavered or blinked. I could find no refuge from this disturbing and penetrating gaze. I could even feel it during the hours of darkness. Eventually he was moved away to another hospital. The gaze I felt at Warblington rather excited my curiosity. I lowered my book and saw Edith looking at me. She was not embarrassed but leaned forward towards me. 'You'll suit a clerical collar,' she said.

A clerical collar! I had no thought or intention of entering the ministry. My hopes were that if I survived the war I could carry on with my naval career.

Edith was one of the most unforgettable persons I have ever met. Gentle and caring, she moved among us like a mother hen. She was a millionairess but also a treasure beyond price. She was a widow; a merry widow in the nicest sense. She had one son who was serving with the RAF at a nearby base for fighter planes. Hoping to offer to him and his fellow pilots some degree of comfort and homely surroundings, she had leased Warblington House from the Marquis of Tavistock. The RAF turned down the offer on the grounds that the house was too far from the airfield and that pilots there were daily expected to 'scramble'. So Edith offered the accommodation to the Royal Navy and we were the first officers fortunate enough to be sent there.

'How do you know that I'll suit a clerical collar?' I asked Edith, 'I never expect to wear one unless perchance at a fancy dress occasion.'

'Because I've just seen one build up around your neck, and you certainly will wear one professionally, if that is the right word,' insisted Edith.

'Tell me more,' I begged, intrigued.

'No; not yet,' she teased. I had to wait.

I lost interest in Nelson's boyhood. I wished that the other officers would push-off to their beds before Edith decided to go. They were agonizingly slow in retiring but eventually Mac led the way, no doubt to ponder between the sheets on the fate of flies.

'They've all gone now as you willed them. What do you want to know?' asked Edith.

'This clerical collar business. Are you serious? Are you suggesting that I will be ordained. I've no intention of going into the ministry,' I told her.

'But you certainly will,' declared Edith with emphasis, 'and you'll come safely through the war. You'll worry unnecessarily about your theological examinations but you shouldn't because you will do quite well.'

We had a little discussion about this then I probed what

I termed as her 'mediumship'.

'I'm not a spiritualist,' objected Edith, 'I just happen to have this extra sense of perception.'

'It's a wonderful gift,' I remarked.

'Not at all. In fact I heartily wish that I hadn't got it. I've given up fighting it now but when it first happened I felt terribly unhappy and disturbed about it and did my very best to obliterate it,' insisted Edith.

'When did it begin?', the questions were pouring from me, 'How old were you? Did you see things as a child?'

I forgot the lateness of the hour which was approaching that when graveyards yawn. Edith didn't seem to mind and was quite happy to continue.

'I had my first experience at the age of twenty-one. I had been presented at court and that weekend father gave a reception at our country lodge,' she began.

'That was quite a while ago,' I said ungraciously.

'Well, Queen Victoria was on the throne but I'll keep my age a secret.'

I apologized.

'At this reception I saw a male guest at the far side of the room. He was silhouetted against the sunlight from the window. As I looked at him he seemed to have two heads. I blinked to clear my sight. The extra head seemed to go away and I imagined that it must have belonged to one of the guests that were strolling on the lawn and had probably passed at that moment.

She paused, pondered or perhaps recollected and then went on. 'A certain royal personage came up to my Dad. I curtsied. He took my hand, then chatted to us. Then his royal highness expressed a wish to smoke a cigar and went out to the lawns to do this. The man that I had seen and imagined had two heads came across to us. He engaged my father in light-hearted conversation. As he talked standing alongside me and no longer silhouetted, another head definitely began to form over his sholder. I saw it clearly and felt startled when I realized that no one else could see it.'

'Was it a man's head? Was it attached to him?' I was still full of questions.

'It was a man's head. It wore a beard and was kindly. It was behind the man but I saw no attached body,' said Edith.

'You know; I really don't understand why I am so interested apart from your prediction of my future ordination. In truth, I'm fascinated,' I said. Edith commented on the lateness of the hour and promised to tell me more the following evening.

I went up to my bedroom. Rumour had it that this room was last occupied by Lord Haw-Haw alias William Joyce the traitor who was hanged after the war. The following morning Edith predicted that I would marry someone with the initial 'E'. She also told me that Ethel wore a pendant around her neck containing a bee's wing. I didn't know of this and had to write to Ethel to confirm it. Edith was right again.

After a day of leaping into and out of landing craft, of incessant rain and the equally incessant invectives of the commander, it was a pleasant experience to relax in the luxury of a bath instead of one of the uncertain showers at the base. Dinner at least equalled the splendid meal of the previous evening. Robbie went to his room to write to his granny, or so he told us, Mac went out to sort his laundry for attention at the base and Edith and I were alone in the library. 'I was still just twenty-one when I had my second "sighting" as I began to call them,' began Edith.

'I had gone to spend a few days with a relative who was the rector of a country parish in Norfolk. I loved to go there for the wild life was prolific. I also had a little favourite there which had been given to the rector as a curiosity; a three-legged duck.'

'Oh, my twin sister has a three-legged duck. The spare leg doesn't function but trails along amidships,' I informed her, so perhaps such quaint animals are not so scarce.

'On the Saturday morning the rectory cook and I arranged the altar flowers in the church. The cook told me that she rarely had the opportunity to attend services on Sundays as the midday meal had to be prepared.

' "Well, we'll put that right this week," I told her. "If you prepare the victuals tonight and show me what to do then I'll take care of the cooking while you go to church. I'll speak to the rector about it."

'Actually I felt a little guilty as I welcomed the chance not to go to the service. I'd heard the rector preach on several occasions and was neither inspired nor challenged but plain bored,' related Edith.

'Did the cook manage to get to church?' I asked.

'Oh, yes,' said Edith, 'I was the only person left in the rectory. It dated from the early fifteenth century. Originally it was a fortified house and there are not many of those in Norfolk. The huge cooking stove was woodburning and a pile of short logs were stored outside but adjacent to the kitchen.'

Edith evidently loved local history and talked at length about the Norfolk parish. 'It was a tradition,' said Edith getting back to the subject of the house, 'that the incumbent must be an academic of Cambridge University, in whose gift the benefice was. One early rector had carved in a stone above the dog kennel *Cave Canum* – beware of the dog.'

'Could a young society lady cook?' I wondered.

'Oh, yes. Besides I had very little to do as everything had been well prepared. I just had to make sure the pots didn't boil over and the roast in the oven was cooking alright. One important chore, however, had been neglected. The ready supply of logs for the stove diminished and to replenish the stove it was necessary to leave the kitchen, cross a stone-flagged passage to an outside door. It was then that I saw him,' climaxed Edith.

'Him? Another two-headed man?' I asked.

'No,' said Edith, 'I had collected an armful of logs and was about to re-cross the passage when I noticed a man walking towards me from the far end of the passage. The only doors in that passage were the two I had just used. Both ends were cul-de-sacs; solid stone walls blocking any thoroughfare.'

'Was there any light in the passage?' I asked her.

'No artificial light,' she said, 'for two windows allowed the daylight to stream in. What I saw was no trick of the light. The man advanced towards me, hesitated, and then retreated walking backwards until he simply walked through the stone wall.'

'All alone in that old rectory. Weren't you scared?' I suggested.

'No. He was not frightening,' replied Edith, 'and I kept my wits about me. I can remember my first reaction was to deplore the sighting. After that first one at the reception I had hoped that it would never occur again. This vision seemed to warn me that I was going to see others.'

'What was he like?' I asked.

'I kept my wits about me sufficiently to note what he was wearing. He was, in my reckoning, a cavalier of the times of Charles II. He wore no hat or wig but his hair was cropped short. A deep lace collar adorned his neck and his tunic and trousers were of maroon velvet. His boots were long and of brown leather and were turned down at the knee. The article that really caught my attention was his sword and sword-belt. The scabbard was inscribed with scrolls and leaves and the belt was very wide and buckled. I remember that he had lace cuffs and that he held the sword at the hilt to prevent it dragging on the floor.'

I was sceptical. 'You say that he disappeared through a solid wall; sword and accoutrements all disappearing?'

'Yes,' she said, 'before my very eyes. When the rector returned from church I related to him what I had seen. He passed it off as the imaginings of a young girl left alone in an ancient and rambling rectory.'

'That's an interesting story. Did anything else happen?' I asked her.

'Several years later,' she continued, 'the rector left this life to dwell among angels with harps and cavaliers with swords. His widow came to spend a holiday with father at our countryhouse. I met her at the railway station.

' "I'm longing to tell you something, dear Edith, but it will have to wait until we reach your home."

'Over tea she informed me of an extraordinary prologue to my rectory sighting. The new rector had decided to break down the wall at the end of the passage to give direct access to the kitchen garden for the domestic staff. This was the wall through which my ghostly cavalier had vanished. In the wall the builders found a stoned-up recess containing the skeleton of a man and a sword and belt. "The new rector, having heard your story from me invites you to go and see the sword before he donates it to a museum," the widow told me.

'I went. The sword I was now looking at was identical to the one worn by my ghostly vision. I would imagine that the unfortunate man had been walled up for some offence no doubt connected with a fair lady or that he had been hiding in those perilous times and had been unable to escape or was found and deliberately incarcerated in that stone tomb,' Edith concluded.

She had a great sense of humour. She told me that she hoped to see all those people she had already seen from the spiritual sphere when she passed on; 'If they are in the right place, I hope.'

Now she's seen, them for the last I heard of her was that she had perished in an air-raid on London.

The Red Sash

Like a tormented soul the engine snorted its restlessness as if eager to cross the great divide into Scotland. Immediately ahead of it was the multi-arched viaduct which spanned the twisting course of the River Aln. The steam released from its cylinders screamed its impatience and disembodied the voice which declared in stentorian tones, 'Bilton Junction; change here for Alnwick.'

Like a thickening plasma the caller came through the hissing steam and was revealed as the station porter.

The guard of the train left his compartment and walked along the platform towards the station master who had just emerged from the booking hall and was dabbing his lips with a large, white handkerchief to remove the traces of tea and beef sandwiches. He assumed a dignified and slow approach towards the guard.

'Hello Jock. There's a few parcels and some mail for Alnwick and a dog in a box for the Duke,' informed the guard. Then bending to the ear of the station master he whispered confidentially, 'See that gentleman alighting?'

'Aye,' responded the station master who hailed from Dunbar.

'It's Charles Dickens,' proclaimed the guard as if

announcing the arrival of the Archangel Gabriel.

'Not *the* Charles Dickens?' doubting Jock replied.

'Yes; the very one.'

The station master squared off his new cap and brushed his uniform with his hands. The station had been opened in 1847 and was still neat and ungrimed. With an air of authority tempered somewhat by a show of deference and humility Jock approached the great author.

'Good morning, sir. Welcome to Bilton. Are you going to Alnmouth?' Jock enquired. Dickens was pleased that his journey was over and he smiled and nodded his head in affirmation. The porter was hovering near in the hope of some reward and he took up the two large handgrips which Dickens had deposited on the platform.

'Can you get me some form of transport to Alnmouth?' the author asked the master.

'Aye, sir; there's a dogcart outside and a flat cart for other passengers.'

'Good. Attend to my bags please,' said Charles as he turned to the porter. The bewhiskered porter deposited the bags in the back of the dogcart and speaking sternly to the slow-witted youth who drove the cart said, 'Drive very slowly and not in your usual madcap fashion. You have a very important personage as your passenger.'

'Who?'

'Charles Dickens,' proudly proclaimed the literary porter.

'Who's he?'

'The author,' the porter informed the youth.

'What's an author?' asked the ignoramus.

Before he could obtain a reply the great man himself approached them. He gave the porter threepence and was assisted aboard. The station master duly entered the arrival of such an august passenger into the station logbook.

The summer light was still lingering as Charles and his beloved Doris strolled slowly across the seaturf towards the long sweep of Alnmouth Bay. Seagulls suppered on the ragworms that betrayed their whereabouts by a shanty town of sand casts. A family of eider ducks pitted their endeavours against an invading sea while the stronger cormorants skimmed the waves towards Seaton Point. The odd puffin, which really belonged to the Farnes, mixed with the arctic terns searching among the low northern ledges of rocks. Charles lifted his eyes towards the south-east. He could see Coquet Island standing guard over the perilous approaches to Alnmouth harbour which unwary mariners might use as a short cut.

'Doris darling, it was a long and sometimes wearisome journey but every mile and every minute was worth it for the reward of seeing you again. Yet I have not made this journey just to see you but to put a proposition to you.'

Charles had given many months thought to the proposition he wished to make and considered that now on the quiet beach on a warm, still evening with the sea gently unfolding upon the golden sands was the ideal time to speak of this matter which was so close to his heart. Without any hesitation Doris intervened.

'No, Charles; nothing like that tonight. It is wonderful to be with you. Let us savour the joy of each other's company and not complicate matters.'

'But Doris . . .' began Charles who had rehearsed this proposal many times as he had journeyed north.

'How long do you intend to stay?' said Doris quickly.

'With your loving permission, for two weeks at least,' replied Charles.

'Then let's wait until later for any serious talk,' she said.

'Very well, Doris. I'll wait an age for you,' Dickens said sincerely. He had known her since she was a child. Her grandfather was related to him in a round-about way and he had called her Dorrit!

They reached the estuary. The sun called it a day and sank beneath the Border hills with a sigh which was borne on the gentle breeze and matched that which escaped from Charles' heart. They paused at an upturned hulk which sketched its keel against a background of Church Hill like a long coping of a roof. Industrious hands had converted it into a home and now an old mariner sat outside the door and rested his back against the tar-swarthed timbers. He sent a curling whisper of smoke from his clay pipe into the still sea-air. Charles was fascinated.

'Do you think that he would let me peep inside his home. I wonder if he can stand upright in it. There can't be much room. Should we ask him?' said Charles.

'Of course. Old Dan won't mind. I've been in several times. He has a wife and young daughter and they love company and a chat. Hey there, Mr Pegg,' greeted Doris. The old man stood up although his legs could not straighten and remained bowed.

'Good evening to ye Mam; Good evening to ye, Sur,' he greeted them, shaking the tobacco from his pipe.

'This is my friend Charles. May we have a peep inside your house? Charles is very much taken with the outside that he cannot imagine what it's like inside,' requested Doris.

'You know the way, Mam; just go in. My wife's busy

getting supper ready,' said Dan.

Doris, Charles and their collie, Ruff, walked slowly back to Doris' home, with Charles a very happy man and determined to visit old Dan's boathouse again.

One fine evening as Doris had not yet returned from an appointment in Lesbury, Charles took Ruff along the sands, again intent on visiting the old hulk. Once again the weather had been kind and the sea shimmered with ten thousand diamonds it caught from the sun. Dan was as usual sitting at the door of his home. Charles joined him and together they chatted.

'Tonight it is so pleasant here but I should imagine the winters are bleak and severe and that you must be very lonely then,' remarked Dickens. 'Are there any ghosts around this place?'

'Aye; it may be lonely at times but I keep myself busy and time passes. It is always warm and snug inside no matter what the weather. No wind will get through these timbers. Ghosts? The village people reckon so. See the hill across the river?' asked Dan.

'Yes' said Charles as his eyes looked towards the bay that swept towards Warkworth.

'That's where the village once stood. The dune is known as Church Hill for the kirk stood there for centuries on the spot where Saint Cuthbert is said to have preached,' related Dan.

'What happened? There's no trace of anything as far as I can see,' asked Charles.

'Years ago a terrible storm combined with extra high tides and torrential rains up the Aln valley caused the river to alter course. The graveyard was stripped of its surface soil and coffins slipped into the turbulence of a doomsday sea while some broke open upon the beach to reveal the shrouded corpses of the dead. The villagers say that they can hear on stormy nights, when the wind blasts in from the east, the agonizing cries of the victims of that storm and that the beach is well avoided,' told Dan.

'Have you seen or heard anything?' asked the author.

'Mebbe I have; mebbe I haven't,' replied Dan as he sucked at his pipe in reflection.

The next evening the fine weather had given way to an overcast sky and Charles and Doris sat in the drawing room, which was on the first floor giving a panoramic view of Northumberland's coast. The maid entered the room, stirred the fire and was about to close the curtains when Charles requested, 'Leave the curtains as they are. Don't shut out the daylight yet.'

The maid withdrew. The couple sat in the fireglow. All seemed to be at peace.

'Dorrit, my little Dorrit, here we are as if we were the only people in the world. What a heavenly place this is; no unrest; no Chartists; no politics or exploitation. It is a veritable Eden.'

Charles was about to feel the bite of the serpent that lurks in every Eden.

'Tomorrow you return to London,' whispered Doris, 'How quickly time has flown.'

'In one way quickly; in another way it has dragged its leaden feet across the sands of time for I have been impatient to speak seriously to you. It has been difficult to curb my impatience but now I can wait no longer. Doris, will you . . .'

'Wait. Let me speak first,' asked Doris and she reached for his hand and held it in both of hers. Her brow furrowed into ridges of concern and for a while she did not speak.

'I have a lover, yes, not only an admirer but one with whom I have made love. I love you Charles, deeply and sincerely but in a different way.'

'No; no; there cannot be another,' protested Charles, 'Say there is no other.'

'There can be and there is,' sighed Doris. 'He is a mariner sailing on a grain ship. He hails from Yarmouth and is at sea now making towards Alnmouth's granaries. He will be here next week and I hope to marry him soon.'

She saw the distress in Charles' eyes. There was a long silence. She leaned forward and kissed his brow.

'I was a coward in not telling you before and I feel ashamed.'

She left the room in distress herself. Charles sat numbed. There had been a storm which had caused the river to change course but now a fierce storm tore at the very foundations of his being; a storm that would alter the direction of his life and to the seeing eye would be seen in his further writings.

He never saw his beloved little Dorrit again. He left early the next morning before she had risen from her bed. When she did she hastened to the large ewer and basin which stood on the marble-topped washstand and was violently sick. She had not told Charles that she was in the early stages of pregnancy and that her evening visit to Lesbury's doctor had confirmed this. The station master faithfully entered the departure of the great man in the station logbook and Charles returned to London.

Much later, on the ninth of June 1865 he was again a passenger on a train but not bound for Alnmouth. It was the Continental Boat train from Dover. On Staplehurst viaduct the train crashed and ten people lost their lives. Charles was shocked and the shock had a lasting effect and left a permanent scar. On the very day of the fifth anniversary of that crash, ninth June 1870, Charles Dickens died at ten minutes past six in the evening, leaving an unfinished manuscript *The Mystery of Edwin Drood*.

But what of Doris? The North Sea tore angrily at the sands of Alnmouth; further out to sea a ship foundered on the east coast of Coquet Island and with its crew perished Doris' lover. In the fulness of time she gave birth to a daughter. She was a pretty baby but was rejected by her now half-demented mother. To avoid the stigma and resulting disgrace of having an illegitimate child in the family the baby was exiled permanently to the third floor attics and was nourished by her grandmother, the sister of a clergyman. The girl developed in beauty and grace but her features remained pale and wan. She never felt the soft breeze upon her face or the kiss of the sun on her cheeks.

Her lungs were never filled with the cleansing sea air of the Northumberland coast. At the age of twelve years she died of tuberculosis.

Today her sad little figure, dressed in a white, lace frock with a red sash about her waist wanders about the attics. She smiles and even now does not leave her prison. She does not frighten, but maybe Doris does. She lies in a suicide's grave at Lesbury.

The Place of Strangers

Rasputin sat in isolation in the shadowed recess of the hotel lounge at Fortingall in Perthshire. His heavy tweed jacket, securely buttoned, hid at least two woollen jumpers. It was the warmest summer for years yet our mad monk added a muffler, a thick overcoat and a woolly hat to his thermal clothes whenever he ventured outside. I am sure that he would be unable to overhear our conversation as his heavy, black beard would absorb any distant sounds and the forest of hairs which sprouted like jungle undergrowth from his obscured ears rendered him deaf to the ordinary sounds of nature.

Alice in Wonderland was also in isolation delightfully arrayed in fancy flimsies which seemed to rebuke the shaggy Rasputin. She counted the flowers fashioned into the design of the chair covers. Blissfully she was always smiling; an innocent abroad and her horizons were of other worlds perhaps with hares and teapots. She was lovely and the Queen of our Hearts.

We had nicknames for all the guests. Colonel Bogie looked military and wore a 'Gunner's' tie but his rank was not quite so elevated and belonged to the Boys' Brigade. We were rather disrespectful about old Bandy. His legs betrayed the fact that he was a pig farmer.

'Well, how did you get on?' asked Ron, from a

sophisticated suburb of South Shields.

'Did you find Pontius Pilate,' further asked his wife Joan.

Pontius Pilate was not a nickname. We could not be so cruel as to wish that nomen upon anyone. Joan was referring to the one-time procurator of Judea.

'I found the ruins of the house of King Metallanus,' I proudly boasted.

'Come now, Jack, tell us how you think that Pontius Pilate was born in Scotland,' asked Ron.

'Because his mother was here at the time.' I bantered and then offered, 'After dinner', hoping that the gourmets would be more gullible then, although I believed the story to be true.

Rasputin had retired for the night afraid that on this warm, balmy, July evening there might be a sudden frost. Alice joined us. The delicious aroma of percolating coffee joined combat with the colonel's Persian cigarette. Full of Eastern promise I began.

'It would have done you lot a power of good to have come with me today. It wasn't too difficult a walk. I went about a quarter of a mile from Fortingall along the road to Aberfeldy. Then I followed the Forestry Commission track up a rather steep incline until I reached the old fort of Dun Geal. Then the going really became tough and I did about half a mile of ridge walking through heather and large stones. Suddenly far from the haunts of men, I found the ruins. They fascinated me. I really felt that I had stepped backwards through time. Everything was so still as if nature was holding her breath as I intruded into the past, yet ever present, peoples of the past. The effort is well worth while.'

'Hold hard, there,' ordered the colonel. 'How did you know about Pontius Pilate and Fortingall?'

'I found out a great deal from the locals and their knowledge of the legend, more from Rob, a graduate of Glasgow University and from the Scottish Records Office. What really got me going is my intense interest in place names. I like to delve into the origin of names and I found that Fortingall means "The place of strangers". Who were the strangers? If one only digs around with a little curiosity and interest it's amazing what one can discover.'

'Carry on, then,' allowed the colonel filling the air with smog.

'King Metallanus, known and loved as Mainus, ruled Central Scotland from 10 BC to 29 AD. I read at the records office that "he was the maist hummull (humble) prince that rang (reigned) above the Scottis (Scots) to his days havand (having) na (no) uncouth or domestik weris (worries) during his tyme". He lived at Fortingall or rather on a prominence near where I've been today.' I described the view from the hill until Alice spoke.

'What was his palace like?'

'No palace, Alice,' I said poetically, 'because his reign was a time of peace he had no need of an elaborate castle to protect him or a splendid palace to impress others.'

Looking out of the windows of the hotel in the fading light we could still make out the outline of the hill opposite and across the river.

'See the far end of that hill where it is at its highest? There was a fort there called Dun MacTuathail. All forts were called "Dun". We now know that hill as Drummond Hill. Metallanus sat secure in the knowledge that he was protected from invasion by a string of such forts and warning beacons which stretched to the east and westward too. Immediately protecting him was Dun Geal, the White Fort. You can see its mound quite clearly from the farm on the roadside.'

'Ron and I passed that farm today. Everyone seemed to be busy working the hay. Next time we go along we'll look for the fort,' said Joan.

'Metallanus would thus have ample warning of the approach of an envoy sent by Caesar Augustus,' I continued.

I paused and sipped the delicious coffee. I didn't want to make the story too long and had to decide what to omit.

'The mission of the envoy really had its roots in the

invasion of Britain by Julius Caesar. He only got as far as what became known as Verulium, nowadays Colchester, and subdued the king of those parts, Cassivelaunus. Before he returned to Rome Julius exacted tribute from the king and his successors to Julius and his successors. It is further thought that Julius took the daughter of Cassivelaunus with him and eventually she became his wife. It's a nice thought that a Briton was the wife of Caesar!'

The top of Drummond Hill was now crowned with the gold of a setting sun although at that time of the year light scarcely yielded to the night.

'The king died and was succeeded by his son Tasciovanus who dutifully continued to pay tribute to Caesar. Eventually he was succeeded by Cunobelinus, immortalized as Shakespeare's Cymbaline. He rather rashly withdrew his tribute payments to Rome and so the Emperor Augustus sent an envoy to apply a little pressure. He was also instructed to journey on to Scotland to approach Metallanus. The "king of the scottis" had ample warning of the approach of the envoy and his Roman escort but it was a peaceful mission and the Roman party was given a clear passage to the king's house. There is no doubt that the king could have exterminated the Romans had he so desired.

'Pontii was the name of the envoy. He came to woo the "humull" prince. Metallanus was told by Pontii that everyone "even the farrest pepill of the Orient" wanted peace, goodwill and friendship with the Roman emperor and sent "sundry goldin crownes and rich jewillis" as tokens of their esteem and if Metallanus was to follow suit then he too would be assured of the friendship of Rome. It was the Roman origin of the Chicago protection racket!'

The name 'Pontii' had alerted my listeners. 'While Metallanus was considering this blackmailing suggestion the Roman party built a camp in which they lived for over a year. This camp is marked on the Ordnance Survey maps as being in the far corner of the field outside here. It was while they were awaiting the decision of the king that a young Scots lass gave birth to a child fathered by a Roman.'

My coffee cup was replenished and I watched the cream circling on the surface. Alice had been listening although her eyes had been following the late flight of the swallows outside as they fed from the myriads of insects that dance and die on a summer's evening.

Her soft, shy whisper asked, 'I love history, but how much of this is fact?'

'So far everything that I have told you is fact,' I asserted, sipping the coffee through the cream.

'Legend has it that this child, undoubtedly born at that time and presumably fathered by a Roman was indeed Pontius Pilate. It is most likely that his father was Pontii from Samnia in southern, central Italy. If so then it is probable that the mother was the daughter of Metallanus who would "lend" the services of his own daughter to such an emminent envoy as Pontii. There is another suggestion that one of the Roman soldiers had a love affair with a local lass and the result was Pontius Pilate. It is interesting to realize that the Menzies family, whose ancient castle is at Weem not far from here, claim descent from Metallanus.'

'Well, that was interesting,' acknowledged the colonel as he rose to leave.

'Sit down; I'm not finished yet,' I invited.

He sat; relit his brown weed and I continued.

'After a whole year the Romans left for home bearing gifts for the "august" emperor. Tradition says that members of Metallanus' family accompanied them and that the child went with them. We do know of a certainty that Menseteus, the eldest son of Metallanus went with the envoy to Rome to present gifts in person. It is further believed that Menseteus heard Christianity being preached at a later date while on what was perhaps his third visit to Rome and was converted. He learnt to read and write while in Rome and returned to Dull to teach and preach.'

'Where is Dull?' asked Ron.

'On the way to Aberfeldy from here but it was then known as Tulli. It is claimed that he founded the first school in Glen Lyon and that his successors were responsible for the foundation of St. Andrew's University.'

'And now to give young Pontii his appendix,' I began.

'Was he born without one?' asked guileless Alice.

'No; no; I mean what we would call today his surname.' Alice was relieved.

'As the son of a barbarian mother, young Pontii would not automatically be given Roman citizenship. At the age of fifteen he would be made a freeman. The insignia of a freeman was a rimless, felt hat known as a Pilatus and so the young lad would then be known as Pontius the Pilatus.'

Ron said to me, 'What are you going to do with all this knowledge you have gained from your research. Preach about it?'

'I've given you only a very brief outline. It's much deeper than this,' I said, 'and I'm going to write a novel, an historical novel, a romance if you like, and I'll call it, *The Place of Strangers*, for that is the meaning of Fortingall.'

'Good,' said Alice. 'If I'm alive when it comes out I'll buy a copy.'

'If you're alive I'll give you a copy,' I offered.

She was so considerate, bless her. She saved me the expense. She died last year!

'It's cool now. Let's have a walk up Glen Lyon,' suggested Ron.

'I think you've walked far enough today,' advised Ethel.

'Oh, I'm OK, and game for a twilight stroll,' I answered. 'The midges have all gone by this time of the evening.'

We turned into the shadowed Glen Lyon reputedly the longest, loneliest and loveliest glen in Scotland. It was known in the times of Metallanus as The glen of crooked stones, and the River Lyon which runs like a jugular vein through the entire length was then known as The Black River.

'What's that?' asked Ron pointing to what seemed to be a stationary, hairy creature. We looked. It was difficult in the fading light to clearly discern anything. 'It's moving this way,' declared Ron, 'stand still. Don't frighten it away.' I couldn't see it moving.

'There are ghosts up here according to legend. One of the McGregors was hunted like a wild beast by the laird and it is said that one can hear his agonized cries as he leaps in ghostly form from crag to crag pursued by baying hounds. He had been detected while risking his life to gain a few cherished moments with the girl he loved, the Laird's daughter,' related Joan.

'I don't know much about that,' I said, 'but I can tell you who joined company with me this evening. I didn't want to tell the others for while I believe I did have a companion, it may have been my imagination working in that strange, quiet and historic setting.'

'When was this, then?' asked Ron.

'On my way to Metallanus' house. I had left the road and found the surface of the track rough and sandy. About a third of the way up I passed into the lee of a copse. It seemed to cut me off from civilization and even from the twentieth century. It was a strange and rather weird feeling almost as if the dark fringe of trees belonged to a far-gone age and I had been transported into it. At first I was bewildered then actually exhilarated. I felt the adventure of it all. I looked up the steepness of the rough gradient and although there was a good climb ahead of me I began to relish the challenge. The ascent took me above the trees and as I looked back I saw another figure toiling up behind me.'

' "Ah; good," I thought, "someone to talk with", so I waited for him. He was small, just about five feet in height. His shirt or tunic was brown and loose and hung outside something that looked like a skirt rather than a kilt. He wore sandals but no stockings. His face was weather beaten but extremely friendly. "I'm going to look for the dwelling place of Metallanus," I said in way of explanation.'

' "I know," he replied softly, "I'll walk so far with you." '

'I began to tell him my theory of Pontius Pilate's birth. He listened, smiled often, nodded now and then but never spoke.

'We reached Dun Geal, the White Fort. He stopped. I

117

had felt the way much easier as I had walked with him.
Time had not existed and the atmosphere had been one of
peace. I had felt that he had truly understood. He was a
patient listener. He stretched out a hand and indicated the
way but he made towards the mound that was once the fort.

' "Thanks you've been marvellous company. By the way,
I'm Jack."

' "And I am Mainus," he said.

'I blinked in astonishment and he had gone!

'I looked towards the fort. A curlew cried from lower
down the hill. I looked down and could see the standing
stones looking very small against the ripening corn; stones
at which Metallanus had worshipped two thousand years
previously. Did he still keep a protecting watch over his
territory? Did he still worship his Wheel-God? Had he just
come from there? Was he buried in Dun Geal or beneath

the ancient Yew tree in the kirkyard which was already old when he was a boy? The questions flooded my mind. I like to think that his caring, noble soul lives on. Whether he was a spirit or the figment of my imagination I shall never know but I do know that he helped me on my way.'

My tale was told. We were back in the hotel telling the tale of the hairy creature. The bar never shut. Rob, the bearded highlander behind the bar explained that the creature we had seen up the glen was a wild cat and for an hour he delivered a lecture on the habits of that animal.

'I have a sporran made from a wild cat's head,' said the proprietor, 'I got it cheap because it's cross-eyed!'

Walking up the Glen the next day Ethel and I saw the wild cat still in the same position. It was a clump of thistles! My Mainus was much more realistic.

Tuesday outing

It was a pleasant room. The sun shone through the large, picture window of the newly added extension. Near to the door stood a modern furniture unit with various bric-a-brac tucked into its shelves, a row of condensed books adding culture and a framed photograph of their benefactor, Aunt Ina, dominating the top. I stood looking at the old lady's features as Carol prepared the coffee. She must have been a happy soul for even though captured on film her smile was still captivating. I felt that I wished I had met her.

I heard the 'bleep, bleep' of Carol's micro-wave oven and knew that the coffee was coming so I settled myself in an easy chair with an adjacent occasional table. I preferred my coffee in a mug and Carol duly obliged providing me with one adorned with a liver bird and the slogan 'Liverpool F.C.' To compensate for it not being a certain north-east team Carol offered me a chunk of cheese cake.

'What was your Aunt Ina's Christian name?' I asked.

'You'd never guess, Jack. It was the same as yours, John!' replied Carol with a smile hoping that she had surprised me.

'John, a boy's name. How come?' I enquired.

'It's quite a silly story, but it took place over eighty years ago. She was my mother's youngest sister,' began Carol. 'My grandparents already had three daughters and grandad longed for a son. "Someone to carry on the family name," he used to say.

'He was a most devout man and felt sure that God would reward his piety with a son as He did for Abraham, Hannah and Zachariah. So in answer to his prayers and his own essential participation in the matter, granny became pregnant for the fourth time.'

Carol laughed, 'Halleluia,' she cried, 'Old Tom had decreed it and it would be so. Remember it was in the days before probes, X-rays and sneak-views. Grandad was certain it would be a boy and while it was still hiding its gender in the security of the womb, grandad always referred to it as John. It seemed as if his prayers were to be answered as grandma went into labour on St. John's Day, December 27th. It was ominous however when her travail persisted overnight and the baby was born on Holy Innocents Day. This little innocent was guilty in grandad's eyes for it was another female.'

I laughed. Carol was a delightful story teller.

'She was six months old before she was baptized on St. John the Baptist Day, June 24th.

' "Name this child," requested the bald-headed vicar whose name was John. Before the godmother could answer, grandad's stentorian voice rattled the rafters of the church with a single syllable, "John".

'The hard-of-hearing vicar asked, "Are you addressing me?"

' "No," came the booming reply, "I'm naming the child."

' "It's a girl," the vicar blundered.

' "You think so? His or her name is John."

'Granny had previously endeavoured to compromise by suggesting a middle name of Elizabeth or amending John to Johnina or Janine but the rock that was grandad was immovable.

'Grandad thinking that there was now no further quality in life or fearing a future shared with a tribe of females, died shortly afterward probably to present his complaint to the highest authority. As she grew up John became known to all and sundry as Ina.'

'That was very interesting,' I remarked, 'and only last month I officiated at the funeral service of a man called Ivy!'

'A man? That was rather awkward for him, wasn't it?'

'He died aged 92 so it didn't do him any harm,' I said.

'Why Ivy?' Carol asked. 'Knowing you, Jack, I'm sure that you would enquire.'

'Aye. His son, now almost seventy, told me that his father was the thirteenth son of an illiterate miner and his wife. They had run out of boys' names so decided to name the boy after their cottage, Ivy Cottage.'

We laughed. 'Let's get back to your Aunt Ina. Didn't she have a tragic death?' I asked.

'Yes,' said Carol, 'and I had a most unusual experience.'

'That wouldn't be unusual for you; you're always having queer things happen.'

'Not like this,' said Carol, 'Ina was a spinster but a very merry one. She was incorrigible! She loved to tease and cast winsome looks at the opposite sex to awaken in the older ones the latent instincts of a hunter which they thought they had lost for ever. How on earth she escaped marriage I do not know. Her most attractive asset was her infectious laugh. When she laughed, all of her laughed. She was a real gem.'

Carol took her photograph from the unit to show me. 'I've been looking at it,' I said, 'she looks lovely.'

'She was as lovely in person as she was in looks and always ready for a lark. Tuesdays were red-letter days for her. It was pension day. Although she had a neat, little bungalow at Ulgham she never lost her Ashington roots and came here every Tuesday to collect her pension. After collecting it at the post office she would cross to the florists to buy me some flowers and take a bus to my home. After lunch I would take her to Newbiggin to her friend's house where they played bridge and her host would always run her home in his car. She just lived for Tuesdays,' said Carol.

The sun came from behind a cloud and shone into the room directly on Ina's photograph as if to remind us that we were talking about her and that she was listening. I had a feeling that, like a stray sunbeam, Ina was sitting in the chair facing me.

'It was a wet Tuesday,' continued Carol. 'In fact it was such a horrible day of driving sleet and cutting winds that I wished that Ina would not be so resolute about her Tuesday trips. Half hoping that she wouldn't come yet knowing that she would allow nothing, literally nothing, to prevent her, I stood at this window watching for the bus. It came and pulled up as it always did for Auntie at the grass verge which is not a bus-stop. As I looked to see if Ina was alighting, my attention was distracted by the flashing blue lights and the strident siren of an ambulance hurrying towards Ashington.

'Then I saw Ina. She was almost at the front door. She was bent forward against the wind and her umbrella was having a tussle with the elements. I hurried to the door.' Carol paused to recollect.

' "Come in, auntie. Let's shut the bad weather out," as the gusting wind sought to cancel out the inner warmth.

'Ina hung her dripping macintosh on the hallstand and carefully placed her umbrella on the wooden surround so as it would not mark the carpet with dripping rain.

'Seated in the lounge she said "Ah, that's much better. Oh dear there's mud on my stockings. Tell me, how are the family?"

' "Have a sherry first, auntie. It'll warm you up. I'll go and put the lunch out on the plates," I said as I left her to

go into the kitchen.

'I was straining the potatoes when I heard her laugh. It made me laugh too. It was a mischievous laugh which arroused my curiosity. What was she laughing about? She had an immense sense of humour and no doubt had something up her sleeve. I hurried to the lounge.

' "Come on, Auntie, lunch is ready. What were you laughing about? Hey, Ina, where are you?" The room was empty. Had she gone to the lavatory? On my way to look I noticed with alarm that her macintosh and umbrella had gone. Beneath the hall-stand rainmarks testified to the fact that her mac had been hanging and draining there. Her umbrella had likewise left a small puddle of wetness.

'I was puzzled. Without any protection against the rain I ran outside. Apart from the passing traffic no one was afoot in this atrocious weather. There was no sign of Ina. I felt numbed and bewildered. Where could she have got to? I went indoors intending to look upstairs when the doorbell rang. Could it be Ina? Had she inadvertently locked herself out? Then the laugh would be on her.

'A policeman stood there, rain dripping from his cape.

' "May I come in?" he pleaded.

'I led the way into the lounge.

' "Is it about Aunt Ina?" I asked but I don't know why.

' "Yes," he said, "would you care to sit down?"

' "What's she got up to now?" I asked, "ten minutes ago she was sitting here and then suddenly disappeared. Look, there's her sherry. She never drank it."

' "No, ma'am; she wasn't here," the policeman said.

' "But she was. I was serving up lunch for both of us. It's all ready in the kitchen."

' "Are you alright, Ma'am? I have some bad news for you," the officer said.

' "Bad news? What about?" I asked feeling further bewildered but not afraid.

' "About your aunt. An hour ago she was crossing from Ashington post office to the florists opposite. Her head was bent low against the sleet and rain and she never knew what hit her. The lorry driver had no earthly chance. It was all over in a split second. We did all we could but she was dead on arrival at the hospital. We found your name and address in her handbag." '

The sunlight now seemed to dance about Ina's photograph. A tease to the end.

Glencoe

A ghost that ate a bacon sandwich! Inconceivable? When one contemplates the land where saints abide forever, the milk and honey and the nectar of the gods, a bacon sandwich seems to be disgustingly mundane. Would the Book of Deuteronomy have to be rewritten? Would the non-pork brigade of Isaiah, Jeremiah and Ezekiel vomit? This ghost was a presbyterian from Scotland and she was hiding in the highlands where anything from haggis to oatmeal passes muster.

I sat in the bar of the hotel sipping orange juice from Israeli oranges in a fashion that would have pleased Delilah and Rahab. I was hoping to please the reapers and sowers, in short, the farmers of the southern climes of County Durham who had been invited to bring their Delilahs along to the talk that I was booked to give. Like me several of the farmers had arrived early and had congregated in the bar. Unlike me they had arrived, poor farmers, in their BMWs; Range Rovers and Daimlers.

'I'm George. This is my wife Linda,' a well-fed son of the soil introduced himself. Linda was suitably well-upholstered and beamed geniality.

'I'm . . .' I began.

'Oh, I know who you are. You're tonight's speaker. Have a decent drink. Whisky?' offered George.

'No thank you. I never drink anything other than orange juice when I'm driving,' I said angelically.

'We are OK. We live only a mile away,' said gin-slinging Linda mistakenly.

'We've read your first book and cannot wait for the second one about the navy. Mark, our son, is in the navy. We'll send it to him. Are you writing any others?' asked George.

'Yes. I'm busy writing a book of ghost stories,' I informed him. There was a pause. Linda looked at George. Their eyes posed a question which Linda answered.

'Yes, George. Tell him.'

'We have told no one of this experience because it is so utterly improbable, so much so that we would not have believed it if anyone else had told it to us,' began George.

'Just a moment. The stories in my book have to be true. Is your improbable story, as you designate it, true?' I asked.

'Absolutely,' affirmed George, 'and we have tangible evidence of it at home to prove it. If you have time tonight after the meeting come round to our home and we'll show it to you.'

I was intrigued but still cautious. I like 'tangible evidence'.

'A couple of years ago we were touring Scotland in our caravan. The weather favoured us for the whole of our holiday. We parked overnight on our journey north in a lay-by in the Pass of Glencoe.'

I know Glencoe well and to me it always has a sinister atmosphere about it even on the sunniest of days. I don't think that I would wish to spend a night among those hills that have now become eternally associated with the massacre of the McDonalds.

'The next morning was glorious. By eight o'clock the sun was above the hills flooding the glen with cheering shafts of light. I filled the kettle and while it was heating walked around the caravan to ensure that all was well,' George said.

'At the back of the van I stooped to check the inflation of the wheel as it appeared to be a little soft. I kicked it and was satisfied. Then I looked around. There was not a soul in sight. I decided to get my binoculars from the boot of my car. About to return to the caravan I was surprised to say the least to see a woman sitting on the grass with her back against the caravan just by the wheel I had examined.'

'Where had she come from,' I asked.

'I don't know. She hadn't been there a minute earlier. She was dirty and unkempt and her clothes can best be described as rags. Yet she had a lovely face which seemed to be so full of life; of peace, yet bewilderment; of pain and sorrow, yet of patient endurance. Her eyes were sad but alert and she gazed furtively about, scanning the hills with concentrated intensity.'

George had set the scene. Now came his revelation.

' "Good morning," I said to her.

' "Good morning," she replied with a definite highland accent.'

George sipped his drink. He now had several listeners as other farmers and their wives grouped around us, but no one interrupted. Linda took up the story.

'I was still in my dressing gown and was brewing the tea when George and the woman came in. I wasn't prepared for a visitor and still had curlers in my hair. I must have looked a sight but she looked worse, poor soul. I wondered what stray he had brought in. Almost automatically I offered her a cup of tea. She took the mug but didn't drink.

' "Would you like a bacon sandwich?" I asked her and went on to explain, "We don't bother much with cooking large breakfasts in the caravan. We're going to have bacon sandwiches."

'She took one. Evidently she hadn't eaten for a very long time for she devoured it in double quick time.

' "Another one?"

' "No, thank you," she replied.'

George took over the story.

'I engaged her in conversation mainly in the hope that I might find out from where she came and to where she was going. I was keen to help her for she looked like a hunted animal. Her next words reinforced this opinion.

' "I've been hiding up here for three months. They'll never find me. No. They'll never find me."

' "If you've been hiding for three months how have you managed to exist?" I asked her.

' "I do sketches and sell them in the Valley of Death.'

'At first I was puzzled, then supposed that she referred to the scene of the Glencoe massacre.

' "I have some with me. Would you like one?" she offered.

' "No. Let me buy a couple from you."

' "I wouldn't sell them to you. You have been so kind. I will give them to you," she said. She passed two sketches over to me and seemed prepared to go.

'Linda asked her if she would like to wash but she rose from her seat rather quickly and made for the door muttering "They'll never find me up here". I accompanied her out of the caravan. She didn't shake hands but clutching her pouch of sketches began to walk away. Linda stood in the doorway and wished her good luck. We watched feeling rather guilty that we had not offered her a lift or insisted that she take money.

'Less than ten yards from the caravan she suddenly vanished. I rubbed my eyes in disbelief.'

George hesitated as if expecting comment from us but no one spoke. He had spoken with obvious sincerity and now no one was doubting him.

' "I don't believe it," I muttered and walked the short distance to where she had apparently disappeared. I looked around. The glen was deserted except for a Dormobile which was just entering the glen a long way off. No other living person was in sight'

'We went into the caravan,' said Linda. 'The two sketches lay on the settee where she had sat. She had not drank her tea but of the bacon sandwich there was no sign.

' "George, go and have another look for her. I feel uneasy. Here, take your binoculars" '

'I searched the area,' said George. 'There was no trace of her. I returned to the caravan. I picked up the sketches. They were neat pencil line drawings of crofts and hills. The woman had signed them with an undecipherable scrawl but the date was clear. May 28th 1692. Two things are significant about that date. First, it was the correct day of her visit to us; May 28th but in the year 1985 and secondly it was only three months after the actual massacre which had occurred on February 13th, 1692. Was she a fugitive from that slaughter? I don't know, but I do know that we entertained her in our caravan.'

When next I'm in Glencoe I will look for her. Art is a hobby of mine. Maybe I'll sketch her . . . in invisible ink, of course.

The bacon sandwich takes a bit of swallowing!

Felix

Noelle had her birthday in September and preferred to be called Carol. She was a nursing sister at a hospital for mental disorders and was regarded by both staff and patients not only with respect but with great affection, for she was truly caring and understanding. She was, however, very matter-of-fact. She was a frequent visitor to the vicarage as a friend of my wife.

'We've a patient in the female ward,' she told me, 'who believes in reincarnation. She is convinced that in a previous existence she was a man. She wants us to refer to her as him and he. She smokes a pipe.'

'I know quite a few women who smoke pipes and even smoke cigars,' I said.

'I don't mind her smoking shag,' said Carol, 'but she spits every few minutes. We've placed a spittoon near to her but she doesn't even try to hit it.'

Ethel and Carol had tea. I had coffee.

'I'd like to seek your advice on a spiritual matter,' began Carol. 'In fact, about a ghost.'

I was rather surprised. She had always seemed to me to be materialistic in outlook and although she often came to church she did not appear to be interested in extra-spiritualistic exercises.

'A ghost? Have you seen one?' I asked.

'Yes,' replied Carol, 'and even you might not believe this. It's a ginger cat!'

'Not someone reincarnated in a different form? Does it smoke a pipe?' I bantered.

'No. Seriously, Jack, there's a ghost of a ginger cat at my friend's house.'

'Where abouts?' I asked. Carol mentioned the small Northumbrian town which is famous for its breed of terriers.

'After going up the hill past the rehabilitation centre there's a new road. To the left where the old road remains is a farmhouse.'

'I know it. Carol, I've been to it before,' I said.

'My friend is not the farmer but is a bachelor who lives in the attached cottage. He lives alone but his sister goes two or three times a week to do his housework,' said Carol.

'Is his name Jamie?' I asked.

'Yes,' affirmed Carol.

'Then I know him. I cannot imagine him seeing a ghost.'

'In fact, he hasn't,' said Carol. 'He seems to be the only one who hasn't.'

'What do you want me to do?' I asked.

'Well, what is it you do to these things? Bell, book and candle?' asked Carol.

'I cannot imagine bell, book and candle being effective or understood by a cat of any hue. Better to try a spiritual mouse if there is such a thing. Seriously, Carol give me the details.'

'Jamie's sister, in the school holidays, took her ten year old son with her when she went to clean up Jamie's cottage. It was a wet day so the lad couldn't very well play among the tractors so he sat indoors watching children's holiday programmes on the television.'

Carol hesitated because a big bumble bee was buzzing in the window; a real one and not an other-worldly one, so Carol was rather a little nervous. She didn't mind spiders or beetles but wasps, bees or flies she abhorred. I opened the window to allow the bee to go out to green pastures and still waters or maybe to be devoured by one of the swallows darting about above the vicarage garden.

' "Mum, isn't this a lovely cat," the boy asked his mother.

' "What cat?" queried his mum.

' "This one on my knee, of course," said the little chappie as he fondled nothing. The mother looked but the lad was stroking thin air.' related Carol.

'Ah,' I interjected, 'the figment of a young lad's imagination. I can remember my eldest son Malcolm had an invisible playmate called Clarence whose hand I had to hold when we were out walking. Paul went even further. He had an army of little men he used to drill.'

'Not so,' said Carol, 'the boy described the cat as a ginger cat and asked if it belonged to Uncle Jamie and could he take it home. Then other people, adults, began to see it including myself. I saw this lovely, large ginger cat with Persian type hair and, I know that this sounds ridiculous, I'm sure that it smiled. I thought of *Alice in Wonderland* but this cat seemed to be so real. The first time I saw it was only for a few fleeting moments. The second time was when I was Jamie's guest at a bridge party. Three of us saw it. It lay, apparently snoozing, under the TV. We tried to pick it up but it just wasn't there. The farmer saw it sunning itself in his flower bed and he thought that it was real. He said that he had never seen such a lovely cat and he bent down to pick it up but it vanished. The flowers were depressed as if by a weight.'

'I suggest, Carol,' I said, 'that we both go to visit Jamie. Can you arrange it?'

'I'll try. The funny thing is I detest cats normally and sneeze when one comes near. I'll get in touch with him and let you know,' agreed Carol. The next morning she rang me.

'Jamie would like you to go up this afternoon if that is convenient to you. I cannot come with you as I am on duty at the hospital. Give me a ring to let me know how you've got on.'

I parked my car on the old road about a hundred yards from the farm. I stood surveying the cottage. It was certainly old and had probably been part of the farmhouse at one time. Then I noticed a young dog, a labrador not fully grown, beside me. I am fond of dogs and stooped to stroke him. It trotted beside me and as I entered the cottage so did the dog. Jamie's sister was there and she had prepared a trolley for our tea.

'I've had a phone call from Carol,' said Jamie. 'She can get along here in about an hour. Should we wait for her?'

'Oh, yes,' I agreed, 'I'm in no hurry.'

We had tea. Carol arrived afterwards. The labrador greeted her with vigour and then lay at my feet.

'That's where I last saw the cat,' said Carol, pointing to beneath the television.

Jamie's sister said to Carol, 'Did you know that I saw it again yesterday? It was about lunch time and it was curled up on Jamie's bed.'

Exorcism time came. The difficulty was that I had no fixed position for this feline phantom; the TV set; the flower bed and Jamie's bed, so we stood in a circle while I prayed.

Was it effective? Evidently yes. As far as I know no one has seen it since then, not even the young lad who would love to see it. I don't know where disembodied moggies go or whether their hunting instincts are dissolved and they live at peace with disembodied mice as the lion will lie down with the lamb. Jamie's ginger cat is probably now in the heavenly ark under the guardian angelship of Noah.

'This is a very friendly dog, you have, Jamie,' I remarked.

'It's not my dog. I thought that it was yours. It came in with you,' Jamie replied.

'It's not mine. I met it when I parked my car and it followed me here. I'm sorry to have brought it in.'

'Not at all,' said Jamie. 'I don't know whose it can be. There is no one around here I know who has a dog like this. They're mainly collies or terriers. He's a well-bred dog, but look, there's no collar.'

After saying my farewells the dog followed me to my car. I patted its head and climbed into the car seat, closing the door. I lowered the window and said to the watching dog . . . 'Go home, boy.'

Was it an exorcism? The dog disappeared!

The Battle of Newburn. 1640

The green fields, the purple moors and the rolling hills of Northumberland and the Borders are a massive patchwork of battle sites where blood has run wild and red, crimsoning the rivers and burns and staining the heather with Scottish and English gore. Even before the times of the Romans, this area rang with battle cries and afterwards, as at Heavenfield, the cries were mingled with prayers.

Once battle is joined, does it ever cease? Legends galore, from Firth of Forth to twix Tyne and Tweed, tell of old battles re-fought by ghostly warriors and sinister horsemen. Often on the windswept moors it is reported that the agonized cries of the dying join with the distant hoot of owls. Flodden is reputed to be re-fought at certain intervals, and I want to tell you of an experience within my own sphere that suggests, if not the actual battle is re-fought, a certain incident which occurred before the Battle of Newburn has never died, and the voices of the dead are once again and often raised in dispute and fatal argument.

As a prelude to my actual experience, let me give you my grand-daughter's story. Julie, at the age of twelve, was instructed by her form mistress to write a ghost story. Being of a sweet, gentle nature her story reflects her gentleness and I feel proud and honoured to include her little story just as she wrote it.

Dear Julie,

I am sad; very sad. The heaviness of my soul may be relieved if I can tell you my story.

I could begin, 'Once upon a time' as my story belongs to the distant past. You may think that your present century has been turbulent. There have been two major wars, strikes, unrest and the terrible tragedy of famine. Let me assure you that your troubled times are little different to any other age. Perhaps one difference is that your wars were mainly fought overseas, whereas my story is involved with civil war.

This country was in the grip of warlike activity. Covenantors, who were especially strong in the Borders and Northumberland, were opposed to those who supported the monarchy. So this area was the scene of many violent and bloody clashes and wholesale slaughter. Families were bitterly split, with fathers fighting against sons, and brothers betraying brothers.

In our lovely backwater there was peace. My home was a large, rambling manor house built in landscaped grounds which swept down to the riverside. Nestling up to us was the township; a collection of neat, small dwellings, mainly cottages and a busy little flour mill and a tannery. The blacksmith had his forge adjacent to the Riverside Inn, a well patronised hostelry on the main highway to Newcastle from Wylam and Corbridge. This was Newburn, so called because a stream of pure, drinkable water wandered from the low hills behind to empty itself above the tidal reach of the Tyne.

I had no brothers or sisters but was well disciplined by my parents who I loved deeply. My own bright bedroom had a view across the river towards another church and village which clung to a dene of dense trees which gracefully curved downwards to form the opposite bank of the river. Near to our house and to the North stood, and still stands, the old village church with a Saxon tower and a pleasant churchyard in which a few sheep grazed. Inside the church our family pew was at the front of the nave. It was high and boxed in so that I could only see other worshippers if I stood upon the hassock. My constant companion was Ranger our golden retriever. He had an endearing nature, soulful eyes and a bushy tail.

The morning had dawned warm and sunny. Seagulls vied with rooks as they gleaned the cornfield. Rose scent drenched the air and the wind held its breath. The joyous sounds of nature's overture, birds whistling, bees humming and the occasional bark of a dog filled the air with harmony and gave no hint of the coming of a bombardment which would rend the peace and destroy the tranquility. A large display of flowers stood on a hall table just inside our door. They were my father's birthday token to my mother two days earlier on the 25th

August.

All seemed to be so peaceful and secure when I heard a strange and fearful sound. It was the roar of a gun cannon. I was alarmed and astounded as well as bewildered. A battle was suddenly being fought on our very doorstep!

Preparations had been going on for this conflict but I was ignorant of such activities. I could not believe or understand what was happening. Startled birds ceased their choruses and flew high. Rooks circled above the church then came down to their own private war against the gulls only to be rudely despatched sky-high as each cannon shot tore through the quiet countryside.

Across the river the opposing forces faced each other. The Royalists had been taken by surprise. They had not previously experienced such a terrifying weapon as the cannon and they quickly abandoned their redoubts and managed to retreat eastwards. There was a lull which lasted until the next morning but on that same forenoon the quiet was again shattered as a thundering knock upon our front door made my father hurry to answer it and me to scurry into the comparative safety of my bedroom. Ranger barked and came with me. Father admitted three travel-stained men into our house. They spoke with a Scottish accent and a rough authority. Father led them into his study. I crept downstairs and slid my trembling hand into that of my father. 'Who are they?' I asked.

In a whisper Daddy answered, 'The leader of the Covenantors, Sir Alex, and two of his senior officers. Don't ask any further questions,' and he hurried back into the study. Mother went into the kitchen to prepare victuals, calling on me to follow. Fear, however, rooted me to the spot and my fear grew as I heard the men engage in a heated dispute. It seemed as if there was a difference of opinion and my young mind could grasp the terms being used; caution, delay, surprise and attack. The angry, raised voices could be heard all over the house. Mother called from the kitchen bidding me to go upstairs again to the sanctuary of my bedroom when, with my foot on the bottom stair and Ranger in close attendance, I heard a shot. In the confined space of our house the shot seemed to be devastating. Ranger cringed behind me as I clung uncertainly to the bannister. Father rushed into the study and saw that an officer had been shot and the officer who had favoured an immediate attack standing white and shaken with a pistol in his hand. Father stooped to tend the wounded man only to find that he was dead. Unthinking, I ran into the room and saw the carnage. Blood seemed to be everywhere and the acrid stench of gunpowder drenched the usual fragrance of the room. The sun disappeared behind a passing cloud and a chill wind of violence and destruction blew like a hurricane upon us.

Father, calm and reassuring, placed his arm around my shoulders as I sobbed in horror.

'Ginny, collect the village children and take them into the church. You'll all be safe, I hope, in there. Once there do not come out until I come for you. Here's my kerchief. Dry your eyes and be a brave lass.'

As I ran from the room with eyes still dimmed with tears I knocked the floral display to the ground. The heavy vase flew through the glass panel of the door. Knowing the love and care that was behind father's birthday gift to my mother, I stooped and lifted the blooms from the floor and carefully laid them neatly on the table.

The village seemed to be deserted and I ran as quickly as my legs would carry me with Ranger running alongside me. A ball from the cannon which had been mounted in the church tower struck the road before me and rebounded to crash into my back. With a sickening thud I hit the ground. Dust was in my mouth and eyes. My legs felt numb. Ranger whined and licked my face. I could not move even though I saw five Royalist soldiers coming furtively towards me. One knelt beside me and lifted my head and offered me a drink from his flask. A tall officer stopped and looked intently at me. There was no pity in his cold eyes only an alertness as he and his men had secretly infiltrated into the Covenantors' territory.

'Did I see you rush from the Manor House?' he asked.

I nodded my head in assent. The pain of such a simple movement ran down my spine like a red-hot poker.

'Tell me; who were the men who entered your home half an hour ago?'

I remained silent.

'Were they senior officers?' he persisted.

I struggled to speak. My throat was closing and I wished to be sick. I felt that I could not betray the men for it might have endangered my father whose sympathies were with the Covenantors.

'I do not know.' My words came slowly, deliberately and painfully.

'But you saw them,' the officer continued entirely ignoring my agony.

'No. I did not.'

The officer consulted with three of his companions then disappeared into our garden. The other soldier gently lifted me in his strong arms and carried me into the church. He laid me on a pew. There were tears in his eyes as he gently kissed me on the forehead. He looked towards the Cross and seemed to utter a prayer. The voice of little children reached me. I longed to see them but my eyes were dim. Suddenly I felt free of pain and was standing in the aisle looking down at my own broken and lifeless body lying grotesquely in the pew.

Why am I sad, now, Julie? The last words I spoke in life were untruths. This has troubled my soul and held me earthbound. Now I feel a change. Telling you my story; unloading my distress, has lifted a great weight from me. I know now that I can go. Mother, Father and Ranger will be pleased to see me.

Julie, thank you for reading this. Can I dare to suggest that in all your difficulties of the twentieth century and onward you go forth into the world in peace being of a good courage and always speaking the truth.

God bless you;

Virginia de Conyers

Hello father!

Julie's story was based on what I had related to her of my visit to Newburn. The tall chimneys of Spencer's steel works indicated that I was within half a mile of my destination. The broad ribbon of Tyne was at low ebb as the extremities of the tidal reach exposed its dark mud. The waters were grey as the sky had darkened prematurely on this winter's afternoon which had threatened a snowfall. Across the water the tall steeple of Ryton church punctured the sky as it rose magnificently above the surrounding trees of the dene. No shaft of sunlight pierced the gloom. The air was still and heavy and the ground as hard as iron.

Jack in the Spirit

Anne's bright, cheerful welcome was in conflict with the chilling elements outside.

'Come in, Mr Richardson. You look really chilled. Take off your coat and warm yourself beside the fire.'

'Call me Jack, please,' I requested.

I removed my scarf, gloves and coat and was about to follow my hostess into the drawing room when I noticed

that a glass panel of the inner door to the hall was shattered.

'Had a mishap?' I asked.

'Not exactly,' was the reply.

There was a moment or two of awkward silence as we stood still. Anne, the vicar's wife, indicated an empty brass vase which stood on a small hall table. Alongside the vase lay a neat bunch of chrysanthemums as if awaiting arrangement.

'Those flowers were in that vase half an hour ago,' she said, 'and with my own eyes I saw them lift out of the vase, lay themselves carefully where you see them now and then the vase hurled itself through the glass panel.'

I was sceptical. I picked up the vase and examined it. There were no signs of impact or scratching but then it was a solid, Indian brass work of art. Heavily inscribed with typical Indian patterns it stood about eighteen inches high.

'Weren't you scared?' I asked.

'Oh, no; it has happened before but so have many other strange things in this house. I'll bring in the tea tray and then if you'd like to hear my favourite story about this old house I'll tell you it over a cup of tea.'

'I don't drink tea,' I informed Anne.

'What then? Coffee, milk or something a little stronger for this winter's day?'

'Coffee, please.'

I settled deep into an enveloping, easy chair. The fire burned cheerfully and seemed to be a mixture of coal and logs. I glanced around to see if there were any brass vases in the room and felt somewhat relieved when I saw that the only possible missile was a brass coal scuttle probably much too heavy for any spiritual weight lifter.

I was to be the speaker at a combined meeting of Mothers' Union ladies on behalf of the Missions to Seamen. I had left my film and projector in my car. The tea trolley creaked in protestation as it navigated the rugs which were scattered about the floor. Teacups clattered as the firelogs crackled. The hot coffee chased away my numbness and Anne began her story of Newburn's contentious ghosts.

'I don't know if you have ever heard of the Battle of Newburn,' began Anne, 'but it took place in 1640, actually on the 27th and 28th of August.'

'Yes; I've heard of it but don't know much about it. The people of Ryton claim that the first engagement took place on Ryton Willows where I used to play football. I've heard a story that after the battle the forces met up again at Blaydon where Major Ballantyne of the Highland Guard ordered 'Blades on', which in modern terms is 'Fix Bayonets' and that the Covenantors won decisively on the hill behind Blaydon as the sun was setting, hence the name of the place is Winlaton. This is all legend and is speculative but apart from these improbable stories I know nothing about the Battle of Newburn,' I replied amazed at my own recollections.

'Let me briefly relate the details, Jack.' resumed Anne who is related to a belted earl, 'The Scottish Solemn League and Covenant army was led by Sir Alexander Leslie of Balgonie. He was a dedicated Covenantor who was willing to risk everything including his life for his cause. A deeply religious man who abhorred bloodshed but who regarded his present campaign as almost a holy war, had come over the Border in great strength to meet an equally strong enemy, the English who were under the command of Lord Conway. I don't know the minute details of the clash but the opposing armies faced each other on either side of the Tyne which in those days was not tidal as far up as here and was fordable in two places.'

Anne is a good cook. Her sponge cake melted in my mouth. I love a good story and listen better on a full stomach.

'The Royalist forces were on the south banks of the Tyne and were concentrated on Stella Haughs with their administration and command out of gun reach on Ryton Willows. The Covenantors were here at Newburn. My story concerns this house. The Scots had hauled a cannon up to the top of the church tower and had lined the north bank of the river with other nine cannons.

'The owners of this house, not then a vicarage, were the Conyers. Sir Roger was sympathetic to the Covenantors' cause. Sir Alexander and his commanders held a pre-battle conference in the room which is now my husband's study.'

'Is that the room to the left of the shattered door panel?' I asked.

'Yes; you can look into it afterwards,' Anne continued. 'Tactics were discussed. Young Major Ballantyne was impetuous and wished to ford the river under cover of darkness.

' "No. We must wait for dawn when we can re-assess the movements and positions of the enemy," objected Major Ian Scott.

' "I disagree," insisted Ballantyne, "delay is fatal and it will give the enemy time to assess our strength and cannon emplacements."

'Sir Alex was about to intervene when Scott called the young major an "inexperienced bungler". Tempers flared. Insults were hurled at each other until both men went for their firearms. Ballantyne won the draw and shot and killed his fellow warrior. The sad thing about it was that they were really good friends and also related through marriage.'

'Such dissension could not have augured well for their campaign,' I remarked.

'It worked out alright for them. The bombardment began at dawn on the 28th August and the Covenantors routed the English,' said Anne.

'Well; where do the ghosts come into this story?' I asked.

'That argument and shot in my husband's study have been repeated most frequently over the years. Our predecessors in this incumbency experienced it too,' began Anne after she had stirred the fire and drawn the curtains.

'Has anyone outside of the vicarage families heard anything?' I enquired.

'We have a new head teacher at our school. She has been here less than a year now,' replied Anne, 'and the vicar told her that she could call on him at any time. "Don't bother to ring the doorbell. It just gets me out of my chair. Just come in and tap on the study door," my husband had told her.

'On one specific occasion she had need to consult him urgently. She entered the hallway and was about to tap on the study door when she heard voices within. She hesitated and thinking that the vicar must be engaged she was about to withdraw when the voices became threatening and abusive. Fearing that my husband was either in danger or about to inflict an injury upon someone she flung open the door to reveal that the study was entirely unoccupied. Not a living soul was in it. Shaken she fled into our kitchen where I gave her sweet tea to calm her down. Even before she told me I knew what had happened, for I can remember the shock I experienced when I first heard the voices.'

'Don't you worry about it? Doesn't it disturb you?' I asked.

'No. You see now that I know the history I know that no one is in any actual danger. Most of our visitors know about it and it never happens at night. The dead just seem to rehearse the drama in perpetuity.'

'Has the brass vase always been involved in these ghostly contests?'

'Not always. In fact this is only the third time the vase has been flung through the panel. Today when it happened there were no raised voices. I think that we will have to replace that panel with wood,' suggested Anne.

'Wouldn't it be simpler just to remove the vase and place it somewhere else?' was my suggestion.

'It might be, but then it may go through a bigger window,' said practical Anne. We finished our tea and the story. Anne left me to wash up and while she was doing that I was alone in the room. The single standard lamp left the doorway in shadow. Hailstones now battered the windows but with less force than a brass vase or at least without such damaging effects. I repaired the fire, the new coal darkening the fireglow. The whole house seemed to creak. The wind whistled in the chimney and caused a cold draught to blow under the door. Did I hear voices? At least one voice had a definite Scottish accent. Suddenly the door was flung open and on the threshold stood a huge man. He was solid enough and was the caretaker of the church hall. Behind him was Anne.

'What plug hae' ye on your projector?' he asked.

'13 amp,' I replied.

'Och, then I'll fix ye up wi' my special adapter as we are 15 amp and round pin here,' he offered.

Again I was left in solitude. The creaking continued and the atmosphere was rather unreal until Anne appeared muffled up in a scarf, woolly hat and heavy coat.

The only power point in the hall was immediately inside the main door. I had scarcely begun to show my film when a latecomer hurried into the room, tripped over my cable, shattered my plug and the caretaker's adapter and plunged us all into darkness.

I finished the evening sitting on a candlelit stage telling ghost stories.

River Patrol

It was January 1906. The tide ebbed. Flotsam of wood, debris and rubbish from the coal ships at the staithes changed direction towards the sea, most of it to be jettisoned on the muddy banks of the polluted river. In the darkness an even darker object floated upon the bosom of the heaving waters. The voluminous clothing of the woman floated about her like a poisonous Portuguese man-of-war but there was no sting in this, only deep mystery. As the greyness of dawn took over from the blanket of night the woman's body was marooned grotesquely on the stone steps that led from the headquarters of the River Patrol to the water. They carried her indoors and placed her on the cold, grey slab upon which future unfortunates recovered from their watery demise would be placed. Hers was the first body to lie there. She had come home!

The chief inspector gave me coffee and arranged for a launch to take me on the river. It was a most pleasant and interesting cruise. I saw warships under construction, merchant ships in dry dock and all floating debris had to be inspected. Oil drums floating on the tide could prove a pollutant if they burst open; and in these uncertain times they could even contain explosives. We saw no floating bodies.

'Well, Jack, you came here to investigate our ghost. I do hope that you enjoyed your trip on the river. I think that it is essential to have an idea of the lay-out of these headquarters if you are to understand our story. I'll hand you over to the sergeant. Bob, are you ready for Jack?' asked the chief inspector.

'Yes,' replied Bob, 'come with me.'

The headquarters lie at the southern end of the oldest bridge spanning the river. From the upper floor we could see the outline of the city opposite; the grey walls of the ancient keep; the lantern tower of the cathedral; the Elizabethan house associated with romantic tales of love and elopement; the less romantic concrete absurdities that serve modern commerce, simply utilitarian and ugly and the tall, dominating floodlight pylons of the main centre of that town's worship; the football ground.

On the landing above the staircase is a spacious set of offices and also two lavatories, one for men and the other, of course, for women. The ground floor is a hub of activity. To the right inside what is now the main entrance is an inspector's office. Opposite there are several rooms including a canteen and a changing room. At the river end of the hallway is a door which at one time was the main entrance but which now leads to the steps that descend to the river.

'This building was opened in January 1906,' said Bob. 'It was constructed on the site of a very old house. This house had to be demolished in order that this one could be built. The family who had lived here for many generations had to be evicted. They made no protest or fuss but seemed to have vanished from the face of the earth. In those days compensation was small and no alternative housing offered. On the very day of eviction the young teenage daughter simply disappeared. The house was demolished in 1901 and this place was not opened until 1906. The day it was opened with much ceremony and pomp the mayor, chief of police, councillors, dignitaries and an admiral had hardly left the premises as the darkness set in when a body was washed up on the steps. It took some time to identify it as the young daughter of the previous occupants.'

Bob showed me some old records which detailed the events of the opening and the tragic return of the girl. Then he went on.

'This affair posed lots of questions. Where had the girl been? In the river? What, for five years? Her body was hardly affected by a stay in the water and it was thought that she had been dead for only a matter of hours when her body was recovered. She still looked like a teenager and the amazing thing was that she had not drowned. The cause of death was never established. Remember they did not have the advanced methods of pathology we have today. But there was the mystery. She was the girl who had been missing for five years. She had not met her death in the river. Why did her body float to this very spot, the threshold of her own home? Why did it return on the day this was officially opened? So I could go on. There are so many unanswered questions.'

'This is an incredible story,' I remarked.

'But even more incredible is the fact that having come home, albeit in death, she has remained here,' said Bob.

'What? Have you seen her?' I asked astonished.

Bob's answer was definite. 'Yes, and more than once.'

'Are you the only one who has seen her. Maybe knowing her story your mind has invented the sightings. I don't mean that you are just seeing things but that mental pictures have sprung from the story.'

'No,' said Bob, 'I saw her before I knew of the circumstances.'

'Who else has seen her?' I probed seeking more substantial evidence.

'We had a new inspector appointed here not long ago. He came from another force and certainly had never been told of the haunting. At five o'clock one evening when most of the staff, both civilian and police, had left except those doing late duties, the new inspector sat in his office near to the main door. The office door was open. Come, we'll go to it.'

Bob led me across the hallway to the inspector's office. 'Sit at that desk, Jack,' he requested me. He then opened the door.

'Now you can clearly see the hallway. Remember it was summer time and daylight. The hallway is quite light. You would be able to see anyone come through the hall,' Bob said. I assented.

'On that evening the inspector saw a young lady enter the premises,' said Bob with police efficiency.

' "Who's that coming in here at this time of the day?" he asked himself. Rising from his chair he went to investigate. The young lady was going up the stairs.

' "Excuse me," called the official, "There's no one up there. Can I help you?"

'Unhurried the woman continued on her way as if she had not heard him so he hastily climbed the stairs after her only to see her disappear into the men's lavatory on the landing.

' "That's the men's" he urgently called and rushing to the door tried to open it. It was locked on the inside.

'He knocked and called until he heard the toilet flush.'

'This is a new one on me,' I informed Bob. 'A ghost who uses a toilet.'

'Well, it happened. I cannot explain it.'

'What happened when she came out?' I asked.

'She didn't. The inspector tried the door again. It was unlocked. No one was in the toilet. There is no window from which one could have escaped. He was not merely mystified but shaken and came down to speak to the duty officer who was in the room opposite his.

' "Yes, sir. That is the spirit of the young lady who was once resident here," the officer reported to his superior and then he told the story.'

'Are the sightings regular?' I asked.

'No,' replied Bob, 'they are not now frequent but she was seen last week. It's a month since I saw her and believe me, Jack, she's lovely and certainly not frightening. The majority haven't seen her but there are six of us here today who have. Can you help her?'

At the moment I've left her in police custody.

Withers' Point

Legends, like good wine, mature with age. The wines become more distinctive to the palate while the legends stimulate and challenge the brain. A good wine ought never to be tampered with but even the most reliable of legends suffers from such additives as rumour, suggestion and expansion. These lie like a heavy sludge often obscuring the original ingredients and distorting the truth that originated the story. Such additions are clearly seen in the stories of Robin Hood and King Arthur. It is frequently difficult to clear away the pollution from the original legend, as many former critics in search of the historic Christ would assert.

The stories of the ghosts at Withers' Point have no doubt been enlarged but once I began my research I found the additives too deeply enmeshed to disentangle without impoverishing the essential content. Withers' Point was well named for even in mid-summer a cold east wind blowing from the North Sea seemed to blight the growth of vegetation. The few trees on this promontory were stunted yet the turf which covered the hard ground was soft and yielding. Gulls stridently squawked about the narrow ledges of the cliff and the smaller arctic terns waded the shallow pools left by the receding tide. Across the shallows the sea was permanently restless as it wrestled with the submerged rocks known as the 'Withers'. The cliffs descended so steeply to the demarcation of terra firma that it had never been possible to construct a harbour below them. The fishing boats which could be seen as fragile little specks about the seascape used the harbour at Craster. Just visible from Withers' Point were the gaunt, forbidding ruins of Dunstanburgh Castle reputed to be haunted by the most unpleasant league of ghosts.

Perilously near to the cliffs stood the now derelict battlehouse. Constructed during the turbulent days of Border forays it had served both as a dwelling house and a bastion. The lower storey was a refuge and byre for livestock while the upper floor served as living quarters.

An outside, stone stairway with its steps now crumbling and unsafe, had led to the main door above the byres. The roof had tumbled in and much of the upper storey walls had fallen away. The lower part of the house is sturdy and well preserved due mainly to its barrel vaulting which was constructed as a safeguard against fire. Now it is a stout, weatherproof refuge for sheep. Across the windswept grass, a hemel stood where it had been for four hundred years and about it farm implements of a bygone age lay rusting.

The modern age was represented by a rather pleasing farmhouse tastefully built to harmonize with its historic surroundings. The few farm cottages would be at least two hundred years old as the outside netties and wash places testified. They were neat and well cared for. Oddly, outside the shepherd's cottage stood a heap of lobster pots suggesting that he supplemented his income by harvesting the sea.

Harry Potts, my friend and on this day my companion, lived in the farmhouse. His family had lived at Withers' Point for centuries from the distant days when there was a sizeable village here.

'Many claim to have seen the ghost of Withers' Point yet I reckon that there is not one ghost but many,' related Harry as we walked from his home towards the battle-house. The September sun was warmer than it was in June yet out of the sunlight one could feel the chilling east wind. We passed by a huge heap of natural manure which steamed like a boiling washpot. The stench was over-whelming.

'Puts hairs on your chest,' said Harry as we involuntarily inhaled.

We reached the battlehouse, and stood contemplating its remains which nature had softened and mellowed.

'There's a nip in the air,' remarked Harry as we stood out of the sunlight. He reached for his hip-flask and slowly partook of a wee nip.

'Have a mouthful,' he invited.

'No thanks, Harry, I'm still tasting that manure heap,' I refused.

The battlehouse despite the autumn sunshine had an air of mystery about it. With little effort one could imagine movements about its shadowed crannies. The cries of the gulls could easily become the agonized or determined cries of reivers, and rogues. The sheep tracks that led towards it had once been trampled by the feet of battle weary contestants, plunderers, rustlers and, so legend declares, even wreckers.

'Once a place like this bleak house is given the reputation of being haunted, the legends increase like snowballs and

ghostly sightings become multiple ' Harry lowered himself
to sit on a stone.

He lifted his eyes towards the stone lintels of the upper
floor door which had stood defiant against the onslaught of
recurring gales which blew with destructive iciness from the
grey waters of the North Sea. The surrounding structure
had yielded to the buffeting and tumbled to the ground.
Moss had softened their chiselled ruggedness and sheep
found in them shelter. Harry continued.

'In the turbulent days of Border unrest, Frank Fenwick
lived here. Although in truth he was a gentle giant he was
renowned for his strength and stature. He was well over six
feet tall, sixteen stones of solid muscle and built like an ox.
He experienced tragedy early in his marriage. When his
daughter was barely six years old his wife endeavoured to
scale down the cliff to rescue a foolish ewe which had
somehow got down to one of the ledges. Black headed crows
joined in the gulls' attacks upon the hapless animal which
in fright might have leapt to its death. Frank's wife slipped
and fell into the fury of the swirling waters below. Frank
had heard the commotion and hurried too late to the scene.
He scrambled down the the waters and entered the sea but
while he could still see his wife's body tossed upon the briny
and could hear her sad cries he could do nothing to save
her. Indeed her body was never recovered.' Harry paused.
His vocal chords needed lubrication.

'Many years later while asleep in his house, Frank was
awakened by his daughter. "Father," she whispered,
"there are men outside. I can hear them."

'Frank crept quietly to the door. Would-be intruders
were endeavouring to draw back the bolt by means of an
inserted knife. Frank instructed his daughter to stand
behind the door and as the knife was withdrawn to push the
bolt quickly and quietly home again.

'Loading his musket he descended to the cowhouse. He
could see one man at the top of a ladder and a group of four
men crouched below.

'With a dramatic bellow this mountain of a man emerged

from the shadows of his own home.

' "You dammed, thieving villains; I'll make starlight shine through some of you." With a thundering roar that shattered that winter's night he shot the lantern holder through the heart. He tore the ladder away from the wall hurtling the unfortunate scaler through the air to meet his doom as his brains splattered the ground upon which he fell. The other men fled, caring more for their own skins than for the fate of their stricken comrades. Frank charged after them like an enraged rhinoceros blundering against a dry wall in the darkness and injuring his leg so much that he had to give up the chase.'

I looked at the empty upper door and tried to reconstruct in my mind the happenings of that eventful night.

'Some say,' continued Harry, 'that on the anniversary of that raid, cries and moans are heard and the spirits relive the grim episode. Others speak of moving shadows while old women claim that Frank's wife returns from her watery grave.'

Harry's feet sank into the turf as I followed him to the old church. Brambles had overgrown the path and the gate stubbornly resisted our efforts to open it.

'Let's climb over the wall,' suggested Harry.

The stout church door emulated the churchyard gate and refused us entry.

'Must be locked,' explained Harry, 'but stay here. I know who has the key,' and with that he hurried away towards the cottages.

This gave me time to look around. I noticed a gravestone incorporated into the lintel of the south door. I rubbed away the lichen and moss from another stone and with difficulty read the inscription. Like many there it related to Harry's ancestors. They had evidently been around when the old battlehouse was occupied. Although there were at least two memorials to the family of Potts predating this particular stone I found that this stone puzled me. With so many premature deaths how was it that Harry came into this world when it appears that like the duck-billed platypus, the Potts were extinct?

> Erected to the memory of
> The Reverend Harold Milburn Potts
> for ten years incumbent of this parish; obit Jany. 18th
> aged 61. 1702.

(The sly old fox, Harry had never disclosed to me that he had ecclesiastical blood in his veins).

> The following offspring of ye above and hys wife Kirsty
> are interred nearby.
> Margaret, obit Feby 21st 1684, aged 10.
> Lance, obit April 31st [yes, the 31st] 1686, aged 17.
> William, obit May 28th, 1686, aged 16.
> Robert, obit June 27th 1689, aged 4½.

> Blessed are the dead which die in the Lord. In the midst
> of life we are in death . . . [indecipherable] . . . trusted in
> Thy mercy.

> Also Elizabeth Kirsty, daughter of ye above parents
> buryd on thys spot obit December 25th 1716, aged 36. [A
> sad Christmas for them] Looking unto Jesus.
> Anne, interred here with her father, obit Jany. 22nd 1722
> aged 38 years.

> Thou hast redeemed me.

> John who was buryd 29th August. anno domini 1693
> aged one.
> Kirsty, spouse of Harold, obit Sept. 5th 1724 aged 82.

Another gravestone caught my eye. In place of a cross there was inscribed a wheel. Had the interred been a wheelwright or did it denote the Creator God? Such a wheel, found on standing stones in the Highlands, often symbolized the sun. Maybe, way back in time the locals

needed the ministrations of Harry's revered cleric fore-
father for their superstitions were legion as I found out in
Harry's tale. Harry returned. The key was massive, at least
a foot long and was secured to a ring which would have
tethered a bull.

The door swung open easily. There was a smell of dank
air and a hollow echo befitting a tomb. The narrow
windows let in little light and I noticed that there were
fittings for oil-lamps. The floor was of heavy flagstones
many of which were worn by the passing of many feet over
the centuries.

'This church was originally built in 1200 on the site of an
older church which in turn had been constructed near to a
burial barrow of Celtic times.' Harry was now the
historian.

'Just look at this font. Believe it or not it was stolen from
Jedburgh.'

'Probably by one of your clan,' I quipped.

'Quite likely,' said the unruffled Harry, 'and this chantry
was added in 1315.'

Harry was a well of information. As we left the church he
led me to a small burn which peacefully lay in quiet pools
until it lost itself and its identity in the Black Tarn.

'This wee burn,' said Harry in his pleasing Northumbrian burr, 'ran red at one time with the blood of both
English and Scots after a fierce battle here. Again, the
locals swear that at times they can hear the battle being re-
fought.'

We wandered to the cliff top. Harry spread his coat over
the turf and we sat gazing towards the Prince of Denmark

beyond the horizon of the sea.

'I must tell you about Archie,' said Harry after a warming sip from his ever handy hipflask. 'He was born here when the village thrived and the church was in constant use; I would reckon about 1784. He used to sit and whittle away at sticks and fence ends. Although in fact a half-wit, his whittling was a work of art and some of his craft can still be seen in the church. He was reputed to be psychic and the church and the graveyard held a special fascination for him. Often he would be seen at midnight among the tombs and graves. He used to enter the church, climb into the pulpit and preach to the denizens of the night.'

'Now, Harry, you promised to tell me of the ghosts that flit between the church and house. I don't fancy sitting here until sundown. So let's hear your grisly saga,' I requested Harry.

Here is Harry's amazing story of intrigue, love, betrayal, killings and spectres!

Moire, known as Mary to the household, was in love. Duggie, the farm hand, was the object of her ardent desires. She was the farm maid and was born and reared in North Uist in the Hebrides. Although now a pleasant and buxom lass, as a young child she had been sickly and frail until the 'wise woman' had passed her through a blazing circle incantating the *Beannachadh na Cuairte* or the blessing of the Circle. This had allegedly endowed Moire with sustained good health but had also bestowed upon her the gift of extrasensory perception. She seemed to be able to peer into the unknown. She came from a family deeply involved in Highland and Island folk lore and superstition. Her father had set aside a 'gudeman's croft'; a small area of land dedicated to the 'gudeman'; in other words Old Nick himself. He had been hauled before the kirk session and accused of 'dark superstition and dealings with the devil'. He had explained that while he was a good presbyterian he had reserved this plot as an insurance against evil powers which could blight his crops and sicken his cattle. As two of the session members also had 'Cloutie's crofts' Moire's father was simply admonished and dismissed.

The day was October 31st, 1806; Hallowe'en to the Borderers; *Samhthain* to the girl. To heighten the significance of the day in the superstitious thoughts of Moire this *Samhthain* coinicided with the crescent moon.

Moire was busy baking her *baonnach samhthain*. It had to be prepared in absolute silence and the baker had not to speak to anyone while the cake was in the oven. In came Duggie.

'Hello love, what's cooking?' She put her fingers to her lips and shook her head. He laughed and teased and tried to make the determined girl giggle. In came Beth, the farmer's wife. She too was buxom and had a happy, friendly nature and loved Moire as a daughter.

'What's going on here?'

'Mary's baking her hallowe'en cake and she mustn't speak while it is in the oven,' replied Duggie.

'Oh, no? We'll see about that,' and Beth joined Duggie in tormenting the hapless lass who was determined to remain silent. Beth seized Moire about the waist and tickled her but without the desired result. All were breathless until Moire bent down to take the cake from the oven. All was well and they all laughed together.

'Tell me, Mary, about your cake,' requested Beth.

'It's a *bonnach*. At midnight I will go to the churchyard and take a bite. Then I will throw the rest of the cake over my shoulder and say, "Here to thee . . . reveal to me," ' the girl replied.

'And what will be revealed?' asked Beth.

'My future. If I am to remain a spinster I will see a woman but if I am to marry I'll see my husband.'

'Are you really going up there at midnight among all those graves . . . and things? It's not safe for a young lass like you to go there on your own,' Beth warned.

'I must go on my own otherwise it won't work and

besides these quarter days are good for drawing lovers together.'

'Better you than me,' laughed Beth. 'I wouldn't be seen dead up there at midnight!'

As she spoke, the girl with second sight shuddered as a cold chill seemed to pass through her.

'Good for drawing lovers together, eh?' said Duggie, the lovesick swain, as Beth unaware of Moire's premonition left the room to the two young lovers.

'Of course it is, especially at the new moon,' asserted Moire.

'How about letting me draw you to me tonight, then?' suggested the lad.

'Oh, yes,' said the equally keen girl, 'after seven in the stackyard.'

The two lovers lay among the hay at the foot of a stack as the sun set and the shadows began to deepen. Moire had previously surrendered her virginity to Duggie and had succumbed again. She did so without any feeling of guilt for in the first place she was very much in love and secondly her father had always advised, 'taste before you eat', and with Moire it was all or nothing, so she extended this principle to embrace all things, even sex. They lay in sweet embrace, exhausted and forgetful of the world about them until the early hoot of an owl brought them back into time from the eternity of love.

'Mary, must you go to the churchyard tonight alone? I'm fearful for you.'

'Yes I want to go and I must go alone as I told Beth. The *bonnach samhthain* will mean nothing if I am accompanied or speak,' replied the girl.

'Won't you be afraid?' asked the anxious lover with protective instinct.

'No. I'll carry a twig of the rowan tree and wrap a red thread around my finger.'

'And do you really think that does any good: It sounds like black magic to me.'

'Of course it's a protection. My father had a rowan tree

trained in the form of an arch over his byre door and he had a trouble-free herd.' replied Moire.

'You're a right witch,' laughed Duggie, 'but I love you.'

He stood up, stretched himself and then in a loud voice declared to the coming night, 'I love her.' Moire stood, embraced him and also, but in a scarcely audible voice, declared her love.

'And I love you. Did I tell you that Beth said that she would speak to Frank about a cottage for us so that we can wed?'

'Mary, that would be marvellous,' said her delighted swain as he kissed her. As they walked back to the farm the crescent moon was declining towards the west thus assuring that midnight would be intensely dark.

'Beth is such a wonderful person that it is rather sad that everyone except her knows that Frank sleeps with the barmaid at the Reivers every week after Alnwick mart,' remarked Duggie.

'I rather think that Beth does know,' replied Moire, 'for I heard the master and Beth having a stormy argument today. I was so worried for he seemed to be going mad. In fact he sounded violent.'

'You heard them rowing?' queried Duggie, 'What was said?'

'I didn't catch everything but I heard Frank say that he would like to get rid of Beth. I've never heard the master shout like that before,' said Moire.

They reached the farmhouse. They embraced and lingered until Duggie had to be about the business of cleaning harness and bedding down the horses. Moire rolled up her sleeves and tackled a mountain of dirty dishes. Frank, the farmer, entered the kitchen.

'Where's the mistress?' enquired an anxious Moire.

His answer was curt and effectively discouraged any further discussion. 'Out.'

By supper time there was still no sign of Beth. Frank seemed to have gone out too. The farm maid kept herself busy until about half an hour before midnight. She peered through the window. The darkness was complete. The sound of the surf beneath the cliff was muffled and the only sounds were those of seagulls disturbed by their own kind. A dim light faltered from the cowshed where Duggie had to sleep and Moire knew that he would not settle down for the night until she had returned safely from the night-encased graveyard. Snugly engulfed in a long woollen coat and wearing a warm, knitted scarf she slipped silently out of the house into the mysteries of the night. The rutted road caused her to stumble frequently. The trees in the copse which served as a windbreak seemed to reach towards her from the darkness with increasing menace and shadows appeared to move and jostle from either side. She left the road and skirted the Black Tarn. Its waters merged into the mysteries of the darkened distance. A startled water hen caused her heart to flutter more wildly than its panic stricken wings. She was a brave and determined girl. She slipped the mitten from her left hand and felt the red thread that was about her finger. Assured she eventually reached the churchyard at that dread hour when it was the undisputed domain of the dead.

The gate was open. She glanced nervously at the headstones and at the grassed over mounds which denoted the long, permanent beds of the perished. She took the little cake from her pocket and carefully and silently unwrapped it. Groping her way to the east end of the church she stood looking around furtively as she felt uneasy now as her confidence ebbed like the tide. It was not her surroundings or that bewitching hour that caused her uneasiness but a sense that there was evil nearby. She waited.

Standing with her feet astride and her head now bared she tried to concentrate her thoughts on the one she wished to marry. She bit at the cake.

She chewed the morsel slowly and deliberately. Then she cast the remains of the cake over her left shoulder and whispered so quietly as if the words were too sacred to be overheard;

'Here to thee . . . reveal to me.'

She peered eagerly though anxiously into the darkness.

Nothing stirred but without a doubt a voice was borne on the wind!

A momentary panic filled her breast. Was a revelation indeed about to be revealed?

She took the sprig of rowan from her coat lapel and holding it before her like some sacred relic or talisman she made her silent way to the south door of the church. She could hear a voice within.

It took a few moments for this Hebridean lass to gather courage.

'It must be Archie. I'll peep in to see if he's in the pulpit,' she decided. Unobtrusively she peered round the doorway.

In the light of candles two men were lowering something into a hole in the floor of the church. Three flagstones were propped up against the nearby wall. The dim light was insufficient to reveal the identity of the men or the bundle they were depositing beneath that hallowed spot.

Terrified, the girl turned to flee. She fell scattering the

gravel beneath her feet. Casting all caution to the wind she fled as fast as her long skirt would allow. Reaching the battlehouse she climbed to the upper floor.

'Beth; Beth. Wake up. Please Beth, help me!' she implored. There was no response for Beth was not there. Distraught she hurried to the cowhouse.

'Duggie,' she shouted into the darkness. A light flickered and a candle was lighted. Duggie caught her as she collapsed into his arms.

'You're shaking, darling. You should never have gone out alone.' he rebuked kindly.

'Oh, where is Beth? I cannot find her,' sobbed the girl with apprehension, 'Duggie, where is she?'

'She'll be about somewhere, maybe even looking for you as she was concerned about you going up to that graveyard at midnight. Come on; we'll look for her,' and putting his arm around her Duggie comforted her.

Despite searching around the farm buildings and the entire upper floor they found no sign of either Beth or Frank.

'I'm fearful for Beth,' said Moire, 'Something inside tells me that all is not well with her.'

'She's big enough to look after herself,' volunteered Duggie. Then the girl stammered out her story of the two men she had seen in the darkened church burying something beneath the flagstones. She shook as she told the story then held tightly to the lad and shuddered.

'Why do you shake like that now? I'm with you,' assured Duggie.

'Because . . . because someone just walked over your grave! What's afoot, Duggie? I feel that there is black evil about.'

'Sleep in my room tonight, Duggie, till morning,' begged the scared lass, 'for I couldn't stay in the house otherwise.'

'Righto,' agreed the lad, 'Now cuddle in. You're safe now and Mary, my treasure, I do love you. I'll speak with Frank in the morning and maybe we will be able to go up to the church and have a look around.'

When morning brought its reassuring light Moire awoke. Duggie had apparently left without disturbing her and would no doubt be busy about the byre.

In fact Duggie was never seen again!

'Frank, where is Beth?' the anxious girl asked the farmer.

'Didn't I tell you? We had a bit of a row yesterday and she's gone to her sister's for a few days. She'll be back when she cools down,' replied Frank.

Time went by. Beth did not return. Moire's heart was torn with utter agony as the days went by and there was no appearance of Duggie. She was afraid to ask about him. Her second sense told her that he was no more, but hope springs eternal though in this case mocked her.

'When's the mistress coming back?' a timorous but loyal maid asked.

'She's not. She has decided to leave me for good. Well, that's her funeral; not mine. She didn't know when she was well off.'

Moire hung her head. She couldn't face the man. She did not believe him. She thought that she knew where Beth was.

'Mary I want you to put clean linen on the bed today. I'm bringing Polly back with me from the mart today. I want you to be nice to her and to do for her what you did for Beth. If you don't or if there is any unpleasantness then you'll have to find another job. Understand?' asked Frank.

Polly duly arrived. All buttons and bows, curvaceous with her breasts displayed to her advantage. Frank fussed over her, shamelessly kissing and fondling her until Moire was so disgusted that she wished to go to her room.

'Where do you think that you're going to, young woman?' asked Frank.

'To my room,' answered the girl.

'Not until you've made Polly her supper. Then clean her shoes and unpack her bag before you go to bed,' ordered Frank.

Polly established herself as mistress of the house. An old man had been employed in place of Duggie and the farmer refused to shed any light on the lad's disappearance.

'He's gone. Good riddance,' said the heartless farmer to Moire, 'and I don't want his name mentioned in this house again.'

After four years Polly gave birth to a baby boy. Frank grew ugly in temper and disposition as if some great weight lay heavy upon his mind. Moire was certain that she knew what that weight was and also noticed that Polly now had little time for Frank and often flaunted him before his fellow farmers. The baby was less than a year old when the faithless mother deserted both Frank and her son.

Moire found it extremely difficult to care for the baby and fulfil all the household demands. Frank seemed to be frustrated and rarely went to the mart. He began to drink excessively.

'I can't do both jobs, Frank. Can you get Polly back?' asked Moire.

'No. That bitch is living in Alnwick with the carrier. She can rot in hell rather than return here. I'll see if I can get someone to look after the bairn at the next hirings,' he promised.

The month of May brought the hirings. Moire made her yearly trip to Alnwick dressed in her sombre Sunday best. She enjoyed looking around the shops and stalls and she ate her packed lunch in the Pastures by the riverside. She had the baby with her but he was too young to participate in the merry-go-rounds. She had arranged to meet Frank at the bottom of Clayport at four o'clock. He had brought a four-wheeled cart into town and now it was laden with hay forks, rakes and other farm implements. A woman sat beside him on the bench he had fitted to the cart.

'Jump up, Mary. Put your packages in the back and give the bairn to Mrs Martin. This is Joan Martin, a widow woman, who is coming to look after Jamie,' Frank informed Moire, 'and Joan, this is Mary. She's been with me for years.'

Moire looked at the woman. Her face was heavily scarred and her hair as white as snow. She was sturdily built and

Moire thought that though her eyes were warm and friendly there was a momentary look of alarm in them.

'May I call you Joan? Everyone calls me Mary.'

'Yes, my dear, you do that,' cheerfully replied the new addition to the household.

Over the next few weeks the two women grew closer together. Moire found in Joan a mother figure. She told of the events of Hallowe'en six years previously and how she still lamented both Beth and Duggie.

Moire thought that Frank might enforce his amorous attentions upon Joan but events turned out differently and tragically.

Moire busily tidied up her own room. It was a cheerful room with bright curtains and a bedspread to match them, all bought out of her meagre ten pounds a year wages.

As she worked she heard her room door open. Before she could turn she was seized from behind and strong arms pinned hers to her side. She spun round helpless in her shock and frantic hands tore at her bodice to reach her breasts. Frank was breathless and sweating. He smelt of alcohol. Exposing her breasts he then tried to remove her skirt. She beat him with her hands and kicked wildly. He lifted her and flung her upon the bed leaping upon her. She wriggled to the floor. He swore and jumped from the bed to pin her down beneath his own heavy weight. She was helpless. She fainted.

Before he could accomplish his foul intentions of rape, another figure rushed into the room and plunged a handscythe deep into his back opening it up as the implement was dragged to the base of his spine. He gurgled and died!

Joan wiped the blood from the scythe and then tenderly placed the unconscious girl upon her bed. After dragging the body to the cowhouse Joan returned to revive Moire.

'What happened? Oh, I remember ... Did he ...?' sobbed the girl.

'No, he didn't,' answered Joan.

'Don't let him in again, please. I don't know what I'm going to do. I cannot stay here any longer. Where is he now? He may come back. He has a foul temper and would kill me.'

'He won't come back,' said Joan.

'You seem fairly definite, Joan.'

'Yes. I've killed him.'

'You've what?' exclaimed a startled girl.

'Don't worry, he deserved it Moire,' said Joan. Moire was astounded.

'You called me Moire yet you only know me as Mary,' said the bewildered girl.

There was silence; a long silence and the unbelievable dawned upon her fevered mind.

She looked searchingly into Joan's eyes.

'You're . . . yes; you're Beth,' she almost screamed and for the second time fainted.

Late that evening Beth told how Frank had attacked her after their row six years previously.

'He thought that he had killed me. He bribed two vagrants from a poor law house in Berwick to bury me under the church floor. Fortunately for me something disturbed them and they fled before filling up the hole. I managed to crawl out and for two days I sat or lay in the pews before I was strong enough to fill in my grave and replace the flagstones.'

'It must have been me who disturbed them when I fled as I ran and fell,' said Moire.

'It took years for my wounds to heal and he was unable to recognise me. I'm sorry, Mary, I've no idea what happened to Duggie. Maybe he paid the price for knowing too much. He was a good lad and my heart bleeds for you, Mary. Now it is all over, I hope, we must start afresh. I would very much now prefer to call you by your correct name, Moire.'

'But what are we going to do?' asked the lass.

'They'll never find his body. The farm actually belongs to me. I'll sell up and together we'll return to Scotland. I belong to Argyll. Let's settle there,' suggested the maternal Beth.

Harry and I now stood on the cliff top. Below us the sea ceaselessly waged conflict with the rocky bastions of the shore and white seahorses betrayed the presence of the treacherous, submerged Withers. Gulls perched perilously on almost imperceptible ledges while others disputed their claims as they screeched and whirled. I turned to look back at the ruins of the battlehouse now silhouetted against the sun which seemed to linger in goodbye before submitting to the hills of Cheviot and the enveloping darkness of night. The headstones in the graveyard stood sentinel over the ancient church; the dead jealous of their freehold. Yet no such stone marks the place where Frank is buried and I should imagine that the clean, pure air of the Hebrides blows gently over the last resting places of Moire and Beth.

'Now, tell me whose ghosts haunt this blighted spot,' I asked.

'No one will go near to the old church at Hallowe'en. Some say that Moire returns still seeking her future but all the reported alleged sightings tell of the spectre of a man. It could be Duggie looking for his love but I think not. Surely in the mercy of heaven the two lovers are eternally united where there is no more death, neither sorrow nor crying. The only definite sighting has been of a man walking from the house to the cliff top. I reckon that is Frank,' declared Harry.

'You say "definite sighting". How definite?' I asked.

'Seen by myself,' abruptly answered Harry.

'The women seem to have found rest, I'm sure,' I submitted.

'Yes, but very few local folk go anywhere near the house at nights. All kinds of rumours abound of noises and shadows, yet we in our farm house which is so close to the battlehouse have never seen anything there except the time I saw the apparition which, by the way, seemed to go over the cliff. I think, to put it bluntly, that the fishes ate Frank.'

'He's not under the barn floor, then?' I asked.

'Hardly likely, and I feel that the people here are still as superstitious as Moire. By the way, Jack, do you ever turn over your money when you see the crescent moon?'

An Aawful Story . . . With a Moral

I arrived at Ulgham, pronounced 'Uffam', to preach at the harvest festival. It was a morning service and tea and

biscuits were provided afterwards to revive the worshippers after the marathon that was my sermon.

'Christians; seek not yet repose;
tea and scones will get you back on your toes.'

I had been famished when I arrived there and had made inroads into a bunch of black grapes which had hung from the pulpit and had led me, as the apple did in Eden, into temptation. However, such furtive eating had created the problem of how to dispose of the seeds.

Jim, the vicar, had balanced a cup of tea on his knee and munched at a dry biscuit which showered me with crumby missiles as we talked.

'Jim, I saw a superstitious image in the vestry; a wooden owl. Gone in for nature worship?'

Jim laughed. 'No. That owl is very old. Do you know the origin of Ulgham's name?'

'What I do know is that it is easier to pronounce than to spell,' I replied.

'Ulgham is an old Saxon word denoting a place or valley of owls,' Jim informed me.

Years later a dear, old lady passed away. I was to officiate at her funeral and rode in the first car provided for the mourners. Bob, her nephew, sat behind me giving me valuable sermon material about his Aunt Elizabeth.

'You mentioned Ulgham just now,' said Bob, 'Do you know how it got its name?'

I felt knowledgeable. 'Yes. It's a Saxon word for a place of owls.'

'Maybe so,' said Bob, 'but here is the real story,' and he plunged into an amazing recitation in the Northumbrian tongue which maybe is akin to the Saxon.

The Legend of Ulgham

Noo, listen whilst aa tel ye what occurred some years ago
When aad Nick hisself came up, cavortin' from below
An' feelin' varry peckish like, – the air was bitin' caad
He deeked aboot the country for a tasty lass or lad
Nor was it long afore he spied, when ower Waalkergate
A fine up-stannin pit-lad, a canny bit o' bait.

Wey, spite o' several pit heeds nigh, and aad Nicks canny age
Doon he swept, for aal the world just like a colliery cage
Till openin' his wings in time, he saved hissel a cloot
An' grapped the poor lad aroond the waist in his most awful snoot
Then up in tiv the sky agyen he flapped wi' waggin tail
An' made away to Northward, in a sort of privit gale.

He kenned a vary canny place, ti eat his wrigglin' meal
A dene beside the Coquet, where the caad wind couldn't steal
But lang afore he got there, the victim gained his wits
An' ventured his opinion, wi some mighty tellin' hits

169

Jack in the Spirit

Describin' in full detail aal aboot aad Nicks queer like form
An suggestin' that his father was a glowry laidly worm.

Noo Nickie stud it for some time, becos his gob was full
Til aal the clivor answers that he thowt on filled his skull
An' became enuff, ti tipple up his last remaining sense
An' made him try a sharp retort, ti ease his pride's suspense
But aal that he cud manage was a sort of 'uff-um' soond
Twas just enuff ti lowse the lad, who dropped upon the groond

He fell intiv a leafy bush beside the churchyard waal
An' that broke what waad sartin'ly hev been a varry nasty faal
Then, in the twinklin' of an eye, he lowped intiv the church
Leavin Nick, the ower taakativ' a screechin' at the porch.
By Nick created sumthin' aaful roond yon holy door
But he'd ti haad away defeated, and hungry as before.

So iver since yon day, ye knaa, the folk aboot the place
Hev caaled it Ulgan, so ti remind us on aboot the case
An the aad yin hissel, discoverin' ti his heavy cost
That if a chep won't haad his tongue, his labour may be
lost
But mind, its aaful contradictious like, becos thon lad
Cud only save hissel, by speechifying on like mad.

I stood on the top step anxiously surveying the sky.
'Look,' said Norman the superintendent, 'Jack's praying.'
Indeed I was ... that Old Nick would not pursue his
aerial manoeuvres over this spot until I was safely encased
in a car. Last week I returned to Ulgham to act as bishop's
chaplain at a confirmation service. The wooden owl was
not in the vestry. Had it migrated or become a tasty morsel
for Beelzebub?

The Legend of Ulgham

Now, listen while I tell you what occurred some years
ago
When Old Nick himself came up, cavorting from below,
And feeling very peckish like ... the air was biting cold
He searched around the country for a tasty lass or lad.
Nor was it long before he saw when over Walkergate
a fine, upstanding pit lad; a juicy bit of bait.

Now, in spite of many pit heads near and old Nick's
advanced age
down he swept, for all the world just like a colliery cage,
and opening his wings in time he saved himself a nasty
collision
and grabbed the poor lad around the waist in his most
aweful snout.
Then up in to the sky again he flapped his wagging tail
and made away to northward in a sort of private gale.

He knew just the right place to eat his wriggling meal;

a dene beside the Coquet where the cold wind couldn't
steal.
But long before he got there the victim gained his wits
and ventured his opinion with some mighty telling hits
describing in full detail all about old Nick's peculiar form
and suggesting that his father was an ugly, horrid worm.

Now Nicky stood for it for some time because his mouth
was full
till all the clever answers that he thought of filled his
skull
and became enough to upset his last remaining sense
and made him try a sharp retort to ease his pride's
suspense.
But all that he could manage was a sort of 'UFF-UM'
sound
Twas just enough to release the lad, who dropped upon
the ground.

He fell into a leafy bush beside the churchyard wall
and that broke what would certainly have been a very
nasty fall.
Then in a twinkling of an eye he jumped into the church
leaving Nick, the over-talkative, screeching at the porch.
Now Nick created something awful round that holy
door
but he had to go away defeated and hungry as before.

So ever since that day, you know, the folk about the plac
have called it Ulgham so to remind us about the case.
And the old one himself, discovering to his heavy cost
that if a chap won't hold his tongue his labour may be
lost.
But think, it is rather a contradiction, because that lad
Could only save himself by arguing like mad.

The Ghost Train

It had been over forty years since I had last stood in Glasgow Central Station, when it had, in my opinion, the exciting stench of steam and coal. Then the living engines always seemed to be straining at the leash to be free to meet the challenge of the railroad whether it took them through the glens to the Highlands or over the summit of Beattock towards the land of the sassenachs. Now the unpleasant fumes of diesel oil drenched the air and overhead cables tangled in a maze. There were blue trains, pacer trains and streamlined, double-ended 125s.

On my previous visit I had stood resplendent in my naval regalia with my gas mask slung across my shoulder and had been mistaken for a railway porter by an elderly lady who had rewarded me with a silver threepenny piece. The public had been friendly; all united in a fellowship born of the uncertainty of war. Today they seemed to be segmented into watertight units who were minding their own business.

Not so with Murdoch. I recognised him at once as he stood quietly smoking his briar and watching the world go by. My memory delved up the far-distant days when he and I were together at the naval college. It remains a mystery how he managed to successfully pass the exams for his mind had been constantly centred on the fair sex.

'It's a necessary ingredient of a sailor's life,' he had asserted and passed his exams with flying colours!

Now he wore a Harris tweed suit that bagged at the knees and looked to be pre-war. His battered 'fore-and-aft' hat matched the suit in age and material but his shoes were new and heavy; suitable for stout walking or even climbing although from what I knew of him he would never exert himself except in the pursuit of females. He carried a

knobbly but serviceable walking stick and over his shoulder
was a spacious rucksack.

He and I had eventually ended up at Rothesay with the
submarine training flotilla before the Admiralty parted our
ways and like ships that pass in the night I had never seen
him again until this very moment. 'Hey; Murdoch.'

He broke from his smoke enshrouded reverie and turned
towards me.

'Jack! I cannot believe it. It must be you for there surely
cannot be two like you. What a pleasant surprise.'

'I recognised you as soon as I saw you. You haven't
changed at all,' I flattered.

'Not much,' he agreed, 'but look at this.'

He removed his hat. He was as bald as a billiard ball.

'What the hell!' he laughed, 'You've never seen a bald
headed donkey.'

I removed my hat. My few stray hairs which vainly
endeavoured to disguise my head of skin blew revealingly
as the draught hit them.

'I'm not much better. I'm told it's a sign of brains,' I
remarked hopefully. The next question was obvious and we
asked it in unison.

'Where're you going?'

Murdoch answered first. 'Dalmally.'

'So am I,' my pleasure was undisguised. 'We'll travel
together.'

'I'm first class,' was no surprise from Murdoch who liked
to swim differently to the other fish in the sea, but this
Royal Sturgeon condescended to add, 'but I'll sit with you.'

'No. I'll pay the extra fare then we can perhaps have a
quiet compartment for we have so much to talk about.'

Settled comfortably in the luxury that belonged to the old
rolling stock we began to reminisce. The buffet car
attendant brought us coffee and biscuits.

'Murdoch; are you married?' I asked.

He sucked at his pipe and watched the drabness of the
city yield to the wider expanses of the Clyde before we
turned towards the breathtaking beauty of Loch Long. It

seemed to be an age before he replied in the negative.

'What happened about that lass you had at Rothesay? Christine, if I rightly recollect. She lived at some Point or other. I thought that you were well matched there. She was a bonny lass and I had hopes for you,' I confessed.

'She was a bonny lass as you so rightly say,' replied Murdoch, 'and I really cared for her. Unfortunately her mother, a widow, cared for me and clung to me like a limpet to the utter exclusion of Christine. She followed me everywhere and always got rid of Christine when I visited their home. So Christine and her mother went to battle stations against each other and I retreated to other calmer exploits. It would have been so romantic; the little cottage with a stream running by the front door and the garden path being a wooden bridge. Poor Christine was entirely eclipsed by her mum so I bid them a sailor's farewell.'

'Knowing you I reckon it wouldn't be long before you found solace in the embraces of another,' I said.

He laughed. 'Yes. Morag had no mother. She was a second officer in the Wrens. In brief she took the high road to the Isles and got marooned with a Mcleod.' He sighed.

'So that was that,' I suggested. I should have known better.

'Oh; no. Believe this or not, Jack, I fell in love, really and deeply in love. What a girl. "Bonny Mary of Argyll" I called her but her real name was Ishbel. She had all the virtues and I had all the vices yet, like opposite poles we were attracted to each other.' He was speaking as a man still in love.

'She was my ideal, Jack; I worshipped that girl.' He sighed again.

'She lived on Loch Awe side. We planned our wedding. She went to Glasgow to purchase her wedding dress, caught an infection, probably from a passenger on a tram as there was an epidemic in the city at that time, and returned home with the dress and a fatal illness. She died five weeks before we were due to be married and is buried up Glen Shira on Loch Fyne. I am making my twice-yearly pilgrimage there now. I stay with her brother at the village of Loch Awe.'

The views of Loch Long were beyond adequate description. We eventually stopped at Arrochar. Pulling away from the station the train jerked violently and stopped.

'Must be a kylie on the line,' I laughed.

'More likely to be a haggis. We're getting into their domain now. A fully grown haggis can derail a train,' Murdoch informed me as he stuck his head out of the train window.

'Can't see any trouble,' he reported.

We never found out what was wrong and after a few moments of delay we set off again.

'Why are you going to Dalmally, Jack?' asked my companion.

'Ghost-busting.'

'Ask a silly question and you get a silly answer,' remarked Murdoch.

'I am in fact going to see if I can do anything in the way of an exorcism,' I insisted.

'Why can't the local man do it?' asked an incredulous ex-mariner.

'In fact it was the local minister who contacted me. He has tried but without success,' I answered.

'How did he get your name?' queried Murdoch.

'He had heard me broadcasting on the subject of ghosts. Then he talked it over with the occupants of the haunted premises and they decided to seek my help.'

It was difficult to concentrate on my story as we were passing through countryside of unspoilt and outstanding beauty. At one time we both watched an eagle circling high in the sky. The hills crescendoed to a magnificent fortissimo of high peaks. Horse-tailed water falls spilled themselves into tarns which reflected the blueness of the sky. We stretched our legs towards the buffet car where Murdoch also exercised his throat muscles as he downed a rum.

'Not like Pusser's rum,' he reflected ruefully, 'but good enough to restore the circulation.'

Whether or not it was as good as navy rum didn't prevent him chasing the first draught with a second of like density.

Wiping his lips he said to me, 'Let's get back to the carriage and you can tell me your story.'

I began. 'An old man lived and worked on a croft of about thirty acres. The whitewashed house and buildings were rather dilapidated but this had been the home into which he had been born. If the walls could have spoken they would have told a long story of toil and sweat; yes; and even of blood. At that dreadful time of the eviction of the crofters his forebears had stood firm against government edicts and bailiffs. They won the day and eventually the old man inherited his birthright.'

I paused. Murdoch stoked his pipe into a miniature furnace and through the resultant haze I continued my tale.

'But what was his right? Hard times hit him and others after the First World War and he had to sell the land while still retaining the tenancy. Mark you, the croft was not at Dalmally but down Loch Fyne not far from Inveraray. I've booked in to the Dalmally Hotel.'

'Good. While you are there I'll drop in to have a meal with you,' said Murdoch, 'It's a very friendly hotel. The dining room has a splendid view.'

'Fifteen years ago the land was sold to developers. Thirty acres were to be transformed into a modern, and as it turned out, pleasing housing estate. The old man, whose only companion was his dog, was ordered out of his house and a demolition order was made for the obliterating of that historic, old homestead. Like his ancestors and with commendable courage and a true, Scottish, dour doggedness he fought officialdom. For over a year he resisted until the day the bulldozers moved in. They hailed him from a distance ordering him to come out. The vehicle drivers saw him come out with his old dog slowly following. He walked to the rear of the building. He looked towards the loch and distant Strachur, then stood bareheaded by his fence. No one living knew that his wife lay buried at that spot. He wasn't saying farewell to her but rather telling her that he was coming to her. The foreman of the demolition party, his patience running out, hailed him again. The old man called his dog and together they made a slow but dignified return to the house. Then two shots were heard.

Closing in, the foreman left his vehicle and cautiously opened the door. The old man lay in his bed. His dog was in his arms. Both had been shot.'

'How very tragic,' said Murdoch who was very anti-establishment, 'They had wiped out not only the old man and his dog but a great deal of history; a history that reflected, despite the clan conflicts and massacres, the true story of the patient, enduring toil of the Scots wherein lies the true glory of Scotland.'

Murdoch, as his name suggests, is a Scot.

'What then?' he further demanded.

I resumed. 'A young, married couple with a five year old daughter, Rebecca, recently bought a house on that estate. Unknown to them this very house had been erected on the site of the old crofter's cottage and one bedroom actually covered that hallowed spot that was the grave of his wife.'

The train changed its rhythm as it passed over a viaduct.

'One morning the little girl told her mother that there was a man and a dog in her room. Realizing that young children often have imaginary friends and animals and that their daughter loved dogs they made light of it.

'The situation dramatically changed,' I related, 'One day the mother was making-up her daughter's bed about ten o'clock in the morning. She suddenly felt that someone was in the room. She looked around and saw no-one. Having completed her task she was about to leave the room when she saw an old man and a dog standing inside the window. At first she was not startled as they looked so real and she was about to speak and say something like "My daughter has spoken about you" when they both vanished into thin air.'

'So they want you to exorcise it,' asked Murdoch.

'Not so fast,' I said. 'They waited for a few weeks before

they confided in their minister and only then because the apparitions were becoming frighteningly frequent. The worthy presbyterian went to the house and prayed. The apparition must be deaf because he and his dog still lingered. On two more occasions he returned to repeat his praying but with no effect. The old man and his dog are still in occupation.'

'Do you think that you can do anything?'

'I can but do my best. Already I have unearthed the history of the croft and the story of the old man. I believe that in cases of exorcism one has to approach the spirit with understanding and sympathy and in a personal way. From what I know of the old man's history I'm sure that he must be a reasonable spirit. I can but try,' I assured my friend.

The train reached Crianlarich. While a little shunting

179

was being carried out to detach a container van, we walked on the platform. The atmosphere was one of peace and tranquillity. There was no hustle or bustle. The little cluster of houses seemed to be congruous with their rugged surroundings. To the south we could see the summit of Ben More and the porter identified other peaks for us.

'Are you sceptical?' I asked Murdoch as we resumed the last leg of our journey.

'Certainly not. I had an experience once in your neck of the woods. I had decided to combine a little sea fishing with fresh water trout angling and booked into a small hotel in a delightful harbour village at the estuary of the River Coquet. The pub was called The Woodman.'

'I know it,' I remarked, 'A homely and friendly little inn.'

'After a splendid day's fishing near Rothbury I returned, tired but with a good catch, to The Woodman. I gave my catch to the landlord, had a bath as they didn't have such a luxury as a shower, then went for a drink before dinner.'

Murdoch paused as if contemplating whether or not to proceed with his tale.

'I must stress that what happened next, occurred before I had a chance to even sample my whisky. The very heavy, vintage cash register at the far end of the bar picked itself up to about a foot above the surface of the bar counter and moved slowly to the other end where it was placed carefully not far from where I was sitting.'

He waited for my reaction but I remained silent.

' "How did you do that?" I asked the barmaid.

' "I didn't," she replied in her Northumbrian dialect,

' "It's Frank playing his prank."

' "I can't see anyone else. Who is Frank?" I asked her.

' "Our resident spook! We call him Frank because of the pranks he gets up to," she informed me.

' "Come off it. Its weight was beyond my capability. It would have taken two men to move it."

' "Don't worry, sir," said the barmain, "Frank will put it back when he's ready, and if you are interested I'll call Pauline in to speak to you."

'Pauline was a student who did part-time hotel duties to supplement her grant. She was a happy, pleasant, intelligent, young lady who was studying science and she would be about twenty years old.

' "You want to know about Frank, sir?" she asked me.

' "Yes, please. Have you seen him?"

' "Only a shadow, sir. I had occasion to resort to the staff ladies' toilet. When I got there I sensed another presence. I knew nothing then about Frank. Uneasy, I hurried back to the reassuring company in the bar. This happened a second time but on that occasion I definitely saw a shadow. It moved towards the door which opened for me. I was petrified with fear. I said nothing to anyone then as I thought that they would ridicule me. Shortly afterwards one of the other girls, also a student, came hurrying from the same toilet crying hysterically. She had seen the shadow and identified the shape as that of a man. It seemed to come towards her as if it was about to envelope her. So now we go in pairs when we wish to use the lavatory and we still see the shadow. Then Frank extended his activities to the bar, moving furniture and especially that till. The mistress claims to have actually seen him," concluded Pauline.

' "By the way, sir, he never goes upstairs," Pauline added as a postscript.

'I saw that till lift and move with my own eyes, Jack, so I'm certainly not a sceptic, but even so I try to keep an open mind on the subject.'

We were on our return journey. Murdoch's rucksack was bulging and now he carried an expanding suitcase held together by two leather straps. True to character as I had known him in days of old he was still the inveterate scrounger. He could carry out this exercise as I remember in such a way that the fleeced would think that Murdoch was doing him a favour by taking the stuff.

'How did you get on, Jack?' he asked.

'Alright as far as I know but it will take weeks to confirm that the exorcism has been effective. I hope it is for the young family is such a happy unit. The little girl is lovely

181

and for her age is quite intelligent. She chatted away with me about the old man and his dog. I had to explain to her in very simple terms that God had a place for them in heaven.'

' "Could the dog stay with me?" she had asked with wide eyes that pleaded like those of a spaniel.

' "That would make the old man very unhappy. I think that your mum and dad are going to get you a little puppy. You'd like that, wouldn't you?" '

'Och,' said Murdoch, 'I hope that things go well up there.'

'Let's settle down and talk of the old times rather than of ghosts,' I suggested but as an afterthought added, 'but first I must tell you of a ghost who wasn't.'

'What was it then?'

'Our postman at home is Norman. He's always smart, sports a Van Dyke beard and breeds bull terriers,' I began.

'Usually it's the bull terriers that seek to exterminate the breed of postmen,' suggested my companion.

'Norman was a fount of knowledge. He knew from where our mail came and the identity of each writer. He sympathized with me every Thursday morning during the football season when no dividends arrived from the pools.

' "Good morning, Jack. Here's one you were expecting but it's not a rebate but a demand. By the way I have a story to tell you. Can I pop round some evening next week to tell it?" '

The train was in no hurry to leave the highlands.

'Did he come back to tell you his story?' asked the Scot.

'Yes,' I replied, 'and it is really a humorous story. He has a friend who is in some society that relives old battles. At weekends some of its members patrol Hadrian's Wall dressed as Roman soldiers. Most of them fight the skirmishes between Roundheads and Cavaliers. There are a few who still indulge in serious conflict as cowboys and redskins.'

'Ah, Custer's last stand,' contributed the Caledonian as we reached Crianlarich once again.

'It was the annual dinner dance of this society and it was held in a church hall on the outskirts of Newcastle. Members and guests were required to wear period costumes. Norman went as a Cromwellian sombrely attired in black with a large, starched, Puritan collar and buckles on his shoes and a huge, leather, buckled belt. His friend dressed as a Royalist flamboyantly flaunting frills and laces and wearing a wide brimmed feathered hat.

'Got the picture, Murdoch?' I asked.

'Aye. Quite a couple,' he replied.
Murdoch almost obscured the 'No smoking' sign as he

once again started a bonfire in the bowl of his briar.

'About midnight,' I continued, 'they decided to phone for a taxi to take them home. There was no phone available in the hall so they went to a kiosk which stood by the churchyard wall. The phone was in working order but vandals has smashed the light. Norman ignited the menu and used it as a torch so that they could discern the digits.

'A midnight reveller, happy in his cups but distressed in his bladder decided to relieve himself in the corner created by the wall and the side of the kiosk. He had begun to urinate and had reached the point of no return when he saw two figures in costume of bygone days emerge from the telephone box, apparently carrying a torch. He left a watery trail as he fled leaving the two "ghosts" splitting their spectral sides laughing.'

'That would cure him of drinking I should imagine,' said the rum-loving Scotsman.

All too soon we were back in Glasgow. It had been a happy chance meeting with Murdoch who had made the return journey so memorable for me. I hope to see him again soon.

'Cheerio Jack; keep your spirits up.'